W9-BWY-410

DISCARDED

At Issue

What Is the Impact of Twitter?

Other Books in the At Issue Series:

At Issue

What Is the Impact of Twitter?

Roman Espejo, Book Editor

GREENHAVEN PRESS
A part of Gale, Cengage Learning

GALE
CENGAGE Learning·

Detroit • New York • San Francisco • New Haven, Conn • Waterville, Maine • London

Shelton State Libraries
Shelton State Community College

Elizabeth Des Chenes, *Director, Publishing Solutions*

© 2013 Greenhaven Press, a part of Gale, Cengage Learning

Gale and Greenhaven Press are registered trademarks used herein under license.

For more information, contact:
Greenhaven Press
27500 Drake Rd.
Farmington Hills, MI 48331-3535
Or you can visit our Internet site at gale.cengage.com

ALL RIGHTS RESERVED.
No part of this work covered by the copyright herein may be reproduced, transmitted, stored, or used in any form or by any means graphic, electronic, or mechanical, including but not limited to photocopying, recording, scanning, digitizing, taping, Web distribution, information networks, or information storage and retrieval systems, except as permitted under Section 107 or 108 of the 1976 United States Copyright Act, without the prior written permission of the publisher.

For product information and technology assistance, contact us at

Gale Customer Support, 1-800-877-4253
For permission to use material from this text or product, submit all requests online at www.cengage.com/permissions

Further permissions questions can be emailed to permissionrequest@cengage.com

Articles in Greenhaven Press anthologies are often edited for length to meet page requirements. In addition, original titles of these works are changed to clearly present the main thesis and to explicitly indicate the author's opinion. Every effort is made to ensure that Greenhaven Press accurately reflects the original intent of the authors. Every effort has been made to trace the owners of copyrighted material.

Cover photograph reproduced by permission of Brand X Pictures.

LIBRARY OF CONGRESS CATALOGING-IN-PUBLICATION DATA

What is the impact of Twitter? / Roman Espejo, book editor.
    p. cm. -- (At issue)
Includes bibliographical references and index.
    ISBN 978-0-7377-6215-0 (hardcover) -- ISBN 978-0-7377-6216-7 (pbk.)
    1. Twitter--Juvenile literature. 2. Online social networks--Juvenile literature. I.
Espejo, Roman, 1977-
    HM743.T95W53 2013
    302.30285--dc23

    2013000314

Printed in the United States of America
1 2 3 4 5 6 7 17 16 15 14 13

Contents

Introduction

Only 11 percent of teens use Twitter on a daily basis, according to a 2012 report compiled by Business Insider. On the other hand, every day, 51 percent use social networking sites and 68 percent send and receive text messages. Furthermore, 72 percent of teens that have signed up for Twitter claim to never use their accounts. Some commentators even propose that the microblogging service appeals more to grownups as a way of communicating. Andrea Forte, an assistant professor at Drexel University's College of Information Science and Technology, describes Twitter as being more adult in interaction compared to Facebook and other social networks, in which users create profiles with details about themselves and their interests that foster a sense of belonging. "Your identity on Twitter is more your ability to take an interesting conversational turn, throw an interesting bit of conversation out there," she tells *The New York Times*. "Your identity isn't so much identified by the music you listen to and the quizzes you take."[1]

Others contend that as a source of breaking news and current events—such as the first reports of ice on Mars and real-time updates on the 2009 election riots in Iran—Twitter does not generally capture or sustain the interest of teens. "Teenagers are notorious for being terrible at social engagement, voting, and keeping up with the news," asserts Ben Parr, a technology journalist. "While I don't want to typecast an entire age demographic," he adds, "I can say this with confidence: Teens, more than any other age group, care about their friends. It's the continuation of real-life friendship (and the creation of online ones) that has driven the tremendous growth of

1. As quoted in "Who's Driving Twitter's Popularity? Not Teens," by Claire Cain Miller, *New York Times*, August 25, 2009. http://www.nytimes.com/2009/08/26/technology/internet/26twitter.html.

MySpace, Facebook, Bebo, etc." He further explains that teenagers do not seek to generate publicity or promote themselves, which Twitter is tailored for. "Twitter is a huge promotional tool—for businesses, for bloggers, for self-described experts—but teenagers aren't as concerned with these things as a whole."[2] To attract more young users to the site, Parr recommends that Twitter grow itself large enough that youths feel pressured to join and add features and third-party applications that emphasize social circles.

Nevertheless, some experts note that a growing number of teens are gravitating to Twitter precisely because many of their friends and family are *not* on it. "It removes the pressure to post on a Facebook wall where friends of friends may see it, not to mention Mom and Dad. In a sense, Twitter is the privacy from Facebook,"[3] blogs Hessie Jones, vice president of marketing at Jugnoo, a company specializing in social media and customer relations. For instance, not only can tweets be hidden from public view, Twitter users can create accounts under pseudonyms known only to a select few. "I love twitter, it's the only thing I have to myself . . . cause my parents don't have one,"[4] declares seventeen-year-old Britteny Praznik of Wisconsin in a tweet. Observers also propose that there is less social pressure on the site, which is more about telegraphing thoughts, emotions, and ideas in short bursts than socializing and establishing connections, which requires more effort and obligations. Mary Madden, research associate at Pew Internet & American Life Project, states that young people do not worry about "friending everyone in your school or that friend

---

2. Ben Parr, "Why Teens Don't Tweet," *Mashable*, August 5, 2009. http://mashable.com/2009/08/05/why-teens-dont-tweet.

3. Hessie Jones, "Stop Poking Me, Mom! Is Facebook Losing the Teen Privacy Battle to Twitter?" blog.jugnoo.com, March 26, 2012. http://blog.jugnoo.com/facebook-versus-twitter-teens.

4. As quoted in "Teens Migrating to Twitter—Sometimes for Privacy," by Martha Irvine, *Today Tech*, January 30, 2012. http://www.today.com/id/46182268/ns/today-today_tech/t/teens-migrating-twitter-sometimes-privacy/#.UJAvRLQVKA1.

of a friend you met at a football game"[5] on Twitter. Supporting this trend, some statistics on its popularity among the age group are encouraging. A 2011 Pew survey indicates that its use among twelve- to seventeen-year-olds doubled to 16 percent that year from 8 percent in 2009.

Like the social networks that came and went before it, the extent to which young people adopt Twitter—and how they adopt it—is viewed as vital to the success of the relatively new Internet platform. "The teens of today will pave the way and direct how we cultivate and evolve communications," declares Jones. Twitter's other effects and consequences—on political change, journalism, human communication—are also being watched, measured, and analyzed. *At Issue: What Is the Impact of Twitter?* delves into these topics and more, presenting diverse perspectives on whether or not the world can be transformed 140 characters at a time.

5. Ibid.

1

Twitter Is Transforming Social Relationships

Justin Marley

Based in Sheffield, England, Justin Marley is a psychiatrist and chair of the mental health informatics group at the Royal College of Psychiatrists.

Twitter has the potential to impact social relationships in numerous ways. As a form of online communication, Twitter may encourage different groups or socially phobic individuals to interact more or, on the other hand, it may reduce face-to-face contact and diminish verbal and non-verbal skills. Friends and family may use Twitter to update each other more quickly and efficiently, creating more connectedness and affecting how people prefer to spend time with media. The messaging service may also provide new opportunities to understand an individual through their activity on Twitter—their interests, patterns of tweeting, and how they interact with other users.

Having used twitter for a few months now, I've begun to ask myself, 'How could Twitter impact on social relationships?' As this is a young technology, there isn't too much research in this area. At the time of writing, a search of the Medline using the keyword 'Twitter' produced 16 relevant articles (not to be confused with another strand of research into the auditory cortex) with a focus on direct health applications of Twitter. Social relationships can be a proxy marker

Justin Marley, "Could Twitter Impact on Social Relationships?" theamazingworldof psychiatry.wordpress.com, December 5, 2009. Coypright © 2009 by Justin Marley. All rights reserved. Reproduced by permission.

for health, and a number of diagnostic criteria for illnesses refer to impairments in social relationships. Thus, the question of the impact of Twitter on social relationships is a useful one to ask. There are a number of possible ways in which Twitter might impact on people's social relationships, and I have grouped them into broad categories. Most of what is written is entirely speculative, but can be revisited once more research evidence becomes available.

Twitter and Face-to-Face Contact

Twitterers don't use face-to-face contact. They rely on short messages to each other or to a wider audience. People are, therefore, focusing on what the person has to say rather than focusing on their appearance, their body movements or listening to their speech. This changes the dynamics of the interaction. People focus on their own appearance, movements and speech in face-to-face contacts to varying extents because they know that this impacts on the effectiveness of their message. The absence of these cues means that the time spent listening to and speaking (Twittering) with a person may differ markedly from the equivalent face-to-face contact. There are so many ways in which this could occur that it is difficult to generalise. Here are a few examples of how it might change interactions.

- A person might choose to listen to another person for a longer period in the Twitter environment than in face-to-face contact if the other person's accent and attire are markedly different from people who they would usually socialise with.

- People who are anxious around others—for instance, if they have social phobia—might find it more comfortable to 'talk' to other people using Twitter. In this way they might be able to 'catch up' on important social trends that help them to better join the conversations of their peers. This in turn might lead to a levelling of the 'social currency' playing field and may have implications for social inclusion. However, this is speculation and research would be needed to investigate this possibility.

People who follow a lot of Twitters from diverse back-grounds could quickly build up an understanding of lots of people, and this in turn would enable them with 'people knowledge.'

On the other hand, having another Internet technology that uses people's time might mean that they spend much less time with people in face-to-face contact. This has been suggested elsewhere. The premise is that people may become deskilled in using verbal and non-verbal methods of communication in real world interactions. If they are deskilled, then this might have a number of implications. Real-world interactions might take longer, they might occur less frequently or Twitterers might be less likely to be included by their non-Twittering peers. The opposite might also be true, however. Twitterers might develop their own method of communicating in real-world interactions. They might be more efficient in their dialogue, may reference material from the Twitterstream or may think more about what they say before saying it. A Twitter culture might develop which would be easily recognisable allowing the listener to deduce Twitter users from non-Twitter users in casual conversation. Twitter might also be better suited to people with certain characteristics—those that are more comfortable with information technology, those that use other similar methods of communicating (e.g., instant messaging) or those that are more introverted. Twitter might not influence face-to-face contacts at all. Again research will be needed to better answer these questions.

Twitter and People Knowledge

Twitters give people an opportunity to better understand a person—what they like to talk about, their patterns of Twittering, how they interact with other Twitter users. There are a number of possible implications of this.

People who follow a lot of Twitters from diverse backgrounds could quickly build up an understanding of lots of people, and this in turn would enable them with 'people knowledge' that would better equip them for social interactions with people. On the other hand, Twittering offers a limited insight into a person since it represents a relatively small proportion of their activities.

People may follow people in a restricted field of interest and become quickly familiarised with the current topics of discussion. This approach is facilitated by the use of Twitter lists which can identify people in a certain area of interest very quickly, allowing them to be added to a person's Twitter stream.

Twitter does let certain dynamics play out. Sometimes people are insulted at what some Twitterers have said and respond. Alternatively, they might be insulted at what some Twitterers have not said or done (e.g., not following someone who has followed them). Twitter, therefore, offers a microcosm of the real world in which dynamics play out in real(ish) time and where these dynamics can sometimes spill out into the real world. This gives people the opportunity to learn about how people behave.

Twitter could help Twitterers to develop a more refined 'lay psychology' that would not replace study of the relevant discipline, but would instead increase the knowledge level of the general Twitter population. If a person behaves in a certain way, Twitter followers can watch their follower numbers and see if they increase or decrease. It is almost as those they are following live Twitter ratings. In this way, they can see what effects certain actions have on people's willingness to follow. This in turn is raw numerical information that they are using. Although there are no accompanying statistics for changes over a unit of time or per tweet at this point in time, it means that people are getting used to assessing behaviours using numbers. However, not many people may be using this approach or if they are, they may not pay too much attention to it. Additionally, the follower numbers may not be helpful in some instances (e.g., where a high proportion of follower accounts have been inactive).

Twitter users with public streams are communicating in a way which differs markedly from informal face-to-face conversations with friends, and if this is not recognized, it can cause problems.

Again much of this is speculation and will need research to provide accurate answers.

Twitter and Offline Relationships

Twitter could be used to communicate more frequently with friends and family in much the same way as with mobile text messaging. Needing to access desktop computers makes this more difficult than with mobile phones, although it is also possible to use Twitter from mobile devices. Twitter could make it easier to quickly follow what friends are doing in much the same way as Facebook does when the person is running short of time. This approach could also be used by a person to update lots of their friends on events quickly and efficiently again in much the same way as Facebook, and here the use of private streams makes this practical. This means that if friends and family use Twitter, they will be better connected, if being better connected means having timely access to information. This might be expected to benefit relationships and people might prefer to use their 'media' time (e.g., television, radio, Twitter, etc.) to follow their friends' Twitter-streams rather than those of celebrities. This might in turn impact on the relative influence of celebrities in culture and may instead mean that people form relatively small groups that are very well connected. However, the ability of Twitter to enable several streams to be followed simultaneously suggests that the more influential figures are likely to remain so and perhaps become even more influential.

Twitter and Work Relationships

Twitter users with public streams are communicating in a way which differs markedly from informal face-to-face conversations with friends, and if this is not recognised, it can cause problems. On Facebook, there have been cases when remarks have been made about the company that employs the person or where the person has made remarks about work colleagues which have led to their dismissal. This may lead to a much tighter demarcation between work and a person's own activities possibly resulting in a smaller percentage of time being spent talking about work in their own time. Many companies are developing their own social media policies for use by employees. Again research will be needed to clarify how this impacts on relationships with work colleagues.

With so many uses of this technology, it is difficult if not impossible to draw general conclusions about the technology, and as with other technologies, accurate answers will most likely arise in circumscribed applications of Twitter.

Twitter Celebrity

At the time of writing, there are several people with over 3 million followers on Twitter and a number of others with Twitter followers in the millions or hundreds of thousands. This is obviously a continuum which extends from such large numbers to a few friends or family members at the other end of the spectrum. Somewhere towards the upper end of this continuum, there are a group of people who have through the medium of Twitter alone accumulated many tens of thousands of followers. Even those with a thousand or a few thousand followers will have the same experience of having sudden immense popularity thrust upon them. This can change the way that people interact and is true of other media also. As the influence of these people increases, so too does the likelihood that they can be helpful to more people. This might impact on the nature of Twitter exchanges, although research again would be helpful here. Away from the Twitter world however, there may be different interactions with Twitter and non-Twitter users. In interactions with non-Twitter users, the influence that a person has on Twitter may be seen as without merit and that person will have to be able to quickly readjust. Here, the argument is similar to that used previously for face-to-face interactions. If the person is used to interactions in a setting where they have a lot of influence, then they will lose the skills needed in a setting where they have much less influence and may have to use various methods to adjust to this imbalance. Others may choose to capitalise on this influence and transfer it offline and again this might impact on the nature of their relationships. Twitterers may find it easier to form new relationships in the real world if people are familiar with them on Twitter before having met them.

Twitter and Business

A number of businesses have a presence on Twitter, and some have both a large number of followers and Twitter at a prolific rate. People who Twitter in their own time and for social purposes may find that a certain percentage of their 'conversation' is spent listening to business messages. This might also be in the form of spam in direct messages which is in effect little different from spam e-mails. At other times, they might choose to listen to interesting content directly from businesses. A number of business Twitters will market a product, and so Twitterers may find themselves being exposed to marketing messages in a greater proportion of their time. However, the ability to tune out certain Twitterers or simply to follow a select group means that Twitterers have a sophisticated level of control over this experience. If Twitterers do find an increasing percentage of their socialising time is spent listenting to marketing messages, this might impact on their communication skills (because they would have less time for other social interactions), the nature of their accumulating knowledge or it might even increase their opportunities to socialise. Again, this is far from clear, and research would be helpful to find answers to these questions.

Twitter was identified as the top word in 2009 in a Global Language Monitoring Survey as well as featuring prominently in President [Barack] Obama's election campaign, reinforcing the importance of this social media tool. In a recent survey, 28% of Twitter users were over 45 years of age and 55% were located in the USA. The interactive nature of Twitter means that people are not only consumers of information, but are also able to contribute. Thus, Twitter has been used for social good such as in the case of raising funds for charity. Others have written about the possible benefits of Twitter including the effects that it may have on relationships. Like any tool, however, it can be misused, and criminal activities have also been coordinated using Twitter followed closely by police surveillance. It has also been pointed out that Twitter can be a source of a misinformation. One author has suggested that Twitter may 'enhance peripheral attention' and impact beneficially on self-esteem, although it has been argued that full attention is not required for some activities. Professor [Susan] Greenfield has suggested that Twitter and other social media forums may change the hardwiring of the brain and impact on attention and even morals. Critics have asked for evidence of this and this is currently being investigated. The dangers of

uninterrupted prolonged sitting may represent a more significant health association.[1] Strategies for using Twitter vary. For
instance, how many people a Twitterer follows has been di-
chotomised into low relevant numbers versus high non-
relevant numbers. With so many uses of this technology, it is
difficult if not impossible to draw general conclusions about
the technology, and as with other technologies, accurate answers will most likely arise in circumscribed applications of
Twitter. Once the results of such research become available,
they can be applied to improve the effective use of Twitter
and may one day be used for those with recognised difficulties
in social relationships. Twitter is just one of many emerging
social media technologies which solve certain problems, and
there is already talk of Web 3.0 applications.

---

1. More recently research has shown that people using social media have wider social
networks offline than people not using social media.

<p style="text-align:right;">

2

Friends Swap Twitters, and Frustration

Andrew Lavallee

Andrew Lavallee is a reporter for The Wall Street Journal.

Many users of Twitter, which combines instant messaging, social networking, and wireless communication, complain that they feel "too connected," receiving messages at all hours and constant updates from their contacts. Inundated with banal information and details about the lives of others on Twitter, some users resort to "unfollowing" or blocking users, creating separate accounts for limited groups, or reevaluating their use of social networks altogether.

Though she already has a blog, a podcast and a character in the virtual world of Second Life, Kera Richard has recently become obsessed with a new online tool for connecting with friends. For the past three weeks, she has joined the crowds on Twitter.com, a site that invites everyone to answer the question: "What are you doing?"

"I didn't get it at first," said the 32-year-old Randolph, N.J., project manager for a financial services company. "How much information do I really need to let the world know about me?"

But soon she was "Twittering" a dozen or more times a day, broadcasting quick, as-they-happen updates to friends who had chosen to link to her through the service. Topics

Andrew Lavallee, "Friends Swap Twitters, and Frustration," *The Wall Street Journal*, March 16, 2007. Copyright © 2007 by Dow Jones & Company, Inc. All rights reserved. Reproduced by permission.

ranged from her lunch (tomato soup and a pretzel) to work annoyances (a high-pitched buzz from a nearby computer). She sent updates from her office and home computers, and used her cellphone to send posts from her car and a bar at happy hour. "It became addicting very quickly," she said.

Twitter is one of several growing services, including Google Inc.-owned Dodgeball, that tie together instant messaging, social networking and wireless communication. Twitter allows members to use their computers or cellphones to distribute short messages on what they're doing. Each message is limited to 140 characters, but there are no limits on how many messages a user can send. Members specify whether they want to be alerted by a text message on their phones or an instant message on their PCs when friends post updates.

This constant dinging of updates . . . , it really just became totally overwhelming.

Like most social-networking sites, once a person opens a Twitter account they can invite their friends to join or connect with existing members. Each member gets a personal Web page that logs all their posts. Some members limit their networks to a handful of friends while others sign up to receive instant updates from dozens of members.

These services elicit mixed feelings in the technology-savvy people who have been their early adopters. Fans say they are a good way to keep in touch with busy friends. But some users are starting to feel "too" connected, as they grapple with check-in messages at odd hours, higher cellphone bills and the need to tell acquaintances to stop announcing what they're having for dinner.

"I probably started removing people the first week," said Ryan Irelan, 31, a Web developer in Raleigh, N.C., who began using Twitter last year. "This constant dinging of updates," he added, "it really just became totally overwhelming. I don't see how anyone could get anything done."

Forrester Research analyst Charles Golvin, who covers consumer wireless services, said that because sites like Dodgeball and Twitter can be tied to a user's cellphone, they can feel more intrusive than PC-based networks. "There's something about your mobile phone. It's a much more personal device and connection because it's with you all the time," he said.

Twitter was launched a year ago by Obvious Corp., a San Francisco start-up formerly known as Odeo Inc. that also runs a podcasting service. Twitter now hosts more than 30,000 posts a day and has more than 50,000 users, according to Twitter founder Jack Dorsey. The service is appealing because of its simplicity, said the 30-year old, who formerly worked as a software engineer at a courier-dispatch service. "You find a lot of connection in just the simplest, most mundane updates from your friends," he said. Twitter doesn't charge users for the service, though he said it may charge for additional features in the future.

Still, users can incur charges for accessing the services away from their computers. Cellphone customers generally have to pay fees to wireless carriers when they use their phones to send or receive text messages. Individual messages tend to cost about 10 cents each, though carriers also sell unlimited messaging plans for about $15 a month.

[Eric Meyer] and friends found themselves receiving 30 to 40 posts a day from one person musing about what to have for dinner and commercials spotted on television.

Twitter has gained some high-profile members recently, including former Microsoft Corp. blogger Robert Scoble and presidential candidate John Edwards. (A recent Edwards post:

"Left Houston this morning. Holding a community meeting on healthcare in Council Bluffs, Iowa today. Des Moines tonight.")

Twitter's expanding popularity has frustrated some users. "I'm a little annoyed by some of these newbies," said Tara Hunt, a 33-year-old marketer in San Francisco who complains that many users seem to be focusing on quantity over quality in their updates. She blames the influx of new users on Mr. Scoble, a Twitter user who began writing frequently about the service on his blog earlier this year. She removed him from the list of people whose posts she follows, turned off by his frequent notes about the service itself. "He Twittered about Twitter," she said.

"Twitter hate is the new black," joked Mr. Scoble, who is linked to more than 1,000 friends on the site. "Some haters have already come around, but to tell the truth, they do have a good point. Do you really need to know that I'm eating a tuna sandwich for lunch? Probably not, although I've had more than one person come over and join me for lunch because I told where I was hanging out." As a concession, he has created a second Twitter account, called "SilentScoble," where he limits his posts to five a day. A recent dispatch: "It's hard to post less than five posts per day. . . ."

Eric Meyer also had to rethink his online network after experiencing what he calls a "Twitter storm." He and friends found themselves receiving 30 to 40 posts a day from one person musing about what to have for dinner and commercials spotted on television. "Who doesn't have a friend like that, who shows up at a party and just won't stop talking," the 37-year-old Cleveland Web consultant said. "Like I didn't have enough information flowing my way every day." He has since created a second Twitter account, linked to a more limited group of friends.

The "too much information" complaint isn't unique to Twitter. Dodgeball, which lets users in 22 cities send group messages telling others where they're hanging out, has spurred similar issues. Brooklyn Web designer Pete Jelliffe, 26, has de-activated links to friends whose check-ins filled his cellphone with text messages, and has been similarly delisted, he suspects, by an ex-girlfriend. "I've blocked people that, say, signed up and just added me because we were acquaintances," he said. "I guess they liked me more than I liked them, and I didn't care to hear about them that frequently."

After joining Dodgeball, Minneapolis Web developer Jenni Ripley, 33, upgraded her text-messaging plan with her wireless carrier when she exceeded her previous monthly quota of 1,000 messages. She and her friends have gotten flak after sending alcohol-fueled strings of late-night messages to their network, or posting messages from places that aren't identifiable meeting spots (such as her boyfriend's car), which some members say is an inappropriate use of the service. "It's caused a massive amount of drama," she said.

"We get some people who get very chatty," said Dodgeball co-founder Dennis Crowley, who became a product manager at Google when the search giant acquired the service in May 2005. Although it is designed for updates around venues and "rendezvous-style behavior," he said, he avoids telling members how they should and shouldn't use it. But even he switched to "digest" mode, which sends one message an hour to his cellphone, after getting bombarded at the recent South by Southwest Interactive Festival in Austin, Texas. He said the service currently has no revenue, but declined to disclose its future plans. He declined to say how many users Dodgeball has.

Twitter's Mr. Dorsey said his company is fine-tuning the service so that members can specify groups of friends whose updates they receive, though he declined to say when the new features would be available. He defended the site's often prosaic content. "Everyone says Twitter's completely useless, I don't want all this information," he said. "We check in later, and they're complete addicts."

Despite her gripe with Mr. Scoble's posts, Ms. Hunt, the San Francisco marketer, said she's only unsubscribed from a few other people's updates. She doesn't even mind the occasional dinner Twittering, she said. "I'm actually kind of interested in what people are eating."

3

Understanding the Psychology of Twitter

Moses Ma

Moses Ma is a managing partner at NextGEN Ventures + Consulting, a strategic consulting firm in San Francisco.

Exploring the psychology and underlying meaning of Twitter reveals that it meets the psychological and social needs of its users. The automated communication service taps into the evolutionary need for community lacking in modern society, offering the feelings of belonging, connection, and acceptance that involvement in religious and social groups provide. Twitter also addresses the higher-level needs of self-esteem, recognition, and self-actualization. But some critics warn that the widespread use of Twitter may result in harmful neuropsychological effects that shorten attention spans and—through the lack of physical cues and auditory gestures—a loss of empathy. The human brain is highly adaptive, however, and the stress and pressure introduced by this new application will expand its capacities.

Twitter has officially become the next big thing in terms of Internet social phenomena, so I can't resist writing about it . . . just like everyone else. Understanding the psychology of Twitter as a case study helps innovators learn how to better predict and even invent emerging white space market oppor-

Moses Ma, "Understanding the Psychology of Twitter," *Psychology Today*, March/April 27/5, 2009. Copyright © 2009 by Psychology Today. All rights reserved. Reproduced by permission.

tunities. And so, this is an exploration into the existential psychology of and underlying meaning—and meaninglessness—of Twitter, to understand its meteoric rise in the Internet world.

First of all, if you've never used or even heard of Twitter, don't worry, you're not alone. As of now, less than 10 percent of American Internet users actually Tweet, but it's growing like crazy: unique visitors to Twitter increased 1,382 percent year-over-year, from 475,000 unique visitors in February 2008 to 7 million in February 2009, making it the fastest growing social media site in the world.

Essentially, Twitter is an automated service for sharing of short 140-character communications. Why the 140 character limit? So you can send tweets from your cell phone as well as your computer. Pretty much every major celebrity has a Twitter channel, from Britney Spears to Stephen Colbert and John Cleese, as the system has become the promotional channel du jour. In fact, Twitter's greatest challenge is the risk of collapsing under its own weight, as servers crash due to the unprecedented volume of traffic and the complexity of revenue models beckon.

Some feel that Twitter is the killer app for killing time, filling any moment with useless drivel—"*boy, I love lightly scrambled eggs*", "*appletini or dirty martini? reply now to tell what I should order*", "*stop & shop is out of weight watchers brownies, but price chopper has 'em.*" I mean, it's crazy. NYU's Interactive Telecommunications Program even figured out how to get plants to Twitter when they're thirsty!

Most interesting is how the Twitter system acts to fill a deep psychological need in our society. The unfortunate reality is that we are a culture starved for real community. For hundreds of thousands of years, human beings have resided in tribes of about 30–70 people. Our brains are wired to operate within the social context of community—programming both crucial and ancient for human survival.

However, the tribal context of life was subverted during the Industrial Revolution, when the extended family was torn apart in order to move laborers into the cities. But a deep evolutionary need for community continues to express itself, through feelings of community generated by your workplace, your church, your sports team, and now . . . the Twitterverse. This is why people feel so compelled to tweet, to Facebook or even to check their email incessantly. We crave connection.

At its worst, Twitter is an exercise in unconditional nar-cissism—the idea that others might actually care about the minutiae of our daily lives.

Maslow's Hierarchy of Needs

It's useful to dig a bit deeper into our need for community. In fact, *needs analysis* is one of the most powerful tools for inno-vators to understand, which invariably leads to the *meaning* of their products. So let's look at Twitter in the context of Abra-ham Maslow's concept of a hierarchy of needs, first presented in his 1943 paper "A Theory of Human Motivation."

Maslow's hierarchy of needs is most often displayed as a pyramid, with lowest levels of the pyramid made up of the most basic needs and more complex needs are at the top of the pyramid. Needs at the bottom of the pyramid are basic physical requirements including the need for food, water, sleep and warmth. Once these lower-level needs have been met, people can move on to higher levels of needs, which become increasingly psychological and social. Soon, the need for love, friendship and intimacy become important. Further up the pyramid, the need for personal esteem and feelings of accom-plishment become important. Finally, Maslow emphasized the importance of self-actualization, which is a process of growing and developing as a person to achieve individual potential.

Twitter aims primarily at social needs, like those for be-longing, love, and affection. Relationships such as friendships, romantic attachments and families help fulfill this need for companionship and acceptance, as does involvement in social, community or religious groups. Clearly, feeling connected to people via Twitter helps to fulfill some of this need to belong and feel cared about.

An even higher level of need, related to self-esteem and social recognition, is also leveraged by Twitter. Twitter allows normal people to feel like celebrities. At its worst, Twitter is an exercise in unconditional narcissism—the idea that others might actually care about the minutiae of our daily lives. I believe that this phenomena of micro-celebrity is driven by existential anxiety. *I Twitter, therefore I am.* I matter. I'm good enough, I'm smart enough, and, doggoneit, *people like me!*

"We are the most narcissistic age ever," agrees Dr David Lewis, a cognitive neuropsychologist and director of research based at the University of Sussex. "Using Twitter suggests a level of insecurity whereby, unless people recognize you, you cease to exist. It may stave off insecurity in the short term, but it won't cure it."

This leads me to a few other problems I have with Twitter and social activity monitoring in general. First, it makes it much easier for stalkers to follow you. Stalkers give me the willies, and better tools need to be in place to identify those you don't want following your every move. However, in Los Angeles, most people celebrate their first official stalker as a benchmark of success. Second, there is a remarkable loss of focus and presence that comes with the information overload that multi-tasking brings. Twitter is like digital crack that invariably turns you into a *tweetker*—no matter how much of it you get, you'll never be satisfied. If you've ever woken up at 3 a.m. to check your email or read tweets, you know what I mean. You know the cold clammy fingers of existential anxiety.

Self-Actualization via Tweets

A more valuable technology tool for humanity might be *the opposite of Twitter*—an application that removes distractions from life, reconnects you to real relationships and human touch, and helps you find the time to focus on what really matters in life. It's an old joke, *"Second Life, heck! I can't even keep up with my first one!"*

Which leads me to return to the remaining highest level in the Maslovian hierarchy of needs—how people might use Twitter to self-actualize. Currently, there are over 200 marketing gurus teaching about how to use Twitter as a marketing channel. How far behind could the spiritual gurus be? The spiritually ubiquitous Deepak Chopra has a Twitter channel. So does the motivational guru Tony Robbins. Existential psychology theory explains that the core tendency of the self-actualizing person is to achieve authentic being. Can Twitter possibly aid in achieving authentic being, or is it fundamentally "mitwelt"—reinforcing the social and interpersonal aspects of life, and thus a distraction from "eigenwelt"—where the treasure of the self is hidden? What would Rollo May do? What would Heidegger say?

Perhaps this is the highest meaning of Twitter: *it's really just a massive social art project*. It's really nothing more than a fun and immersive conceptual art installation about humanity and by humanity, composed of individual 140 character haikus. (In fact, there's even a name for the perfect tweet haiku . . . *twoosh!* It's when your tweet hits exactly 140 characters and makes that sound. Tweet + swoosh. Nothing but net.) In fact, all the twooshes in the world add up into a giant global pachinko machine, made all the more addictive because Twitter's software designers were clever enough to program in tenacious intermittent reward systems, so you end up like a loser in Vegas, behaviorally trapped at the slot machines of life.

Ask yourself, when you Twitter, are you tweeting like a caged bird or exclaiming your passion and enjoying the *spaciality of existence*? Medard Boss, a Swiss psychiatrist who developed daseinsanalysis and who coined the term, wrote, "Openness constitutes the true nature of spatiality in the human world. I am more open to my distant friend and he is clearer to me than my neighbor is." Isn't that exactly what the openness of the Internet enables—making distant friends clearer than the neighbor next door?

To me, the Twitterverse is like a river of human awareness, composed of billions of tiny 140 character molecules—each a snapshot of life or a thought or a reflection.

Perhaps the key distinction lies in whether you are truly enjoying humanity's meta-haiku, or is the motivation to Twitter actually a fear of being alone? Kierkegaard once said that true heroism is "daring to be entirely oneself, alone before God." Is Twitter actually powered by a global case of monophobia?

Perhaps a more enlightened way to look at it is that you aren't adding to the spam or garbage-in-garbage-out overload, you're really just enjoying a cyber-zen moment of mindfulness to be present and tweet thyself. We're *all interconnected now*— each of us acting like a single neuron in humanity's brain, firing bits of electricity at one another, slowly coadunating and collectively struggling toward a great awakening. That awakening could turn out to be the next stage in our evolution, and a single tweet the butterfly's wings that eventually leads to a big bang of global meta-consciousness.

To me, the Twitterverse is like a river of human awareness, composed of billions of tiny 140 character molecules—each a snapshot of life or a thought or a reflection. A river of pure information that equals energy, according to the laws of quantum thermodynamics and stochastic processes. A river of life flowing by us as we meditate at its bank like some Siddhartha wannabe, in tattered jeans and Oakley sunglasses instead of orchid robes and begging bowl. And now, after long last, *we see.*

We see the beauty of the river, that some now call *ambient awareness.*

We reach in and touch the *water of human consciousness.*

Little eddies form—those are called *tweetclouds.*

We can be one with the river.

Or not.

It's all good. . . .

My Experiment

I decided to jump in and see what it might be like in the deeper part of the river—sink or swim. Well, the current is pretty strong out there. However, Twitter usage manages its own learning curve by matching the numbers of followers and followees you have. A newbie, like me, would normally have only a few dozen follows, generating a post every few minutes. But a heavy Twitter user, with 10,000 follows and followers, might be processing something like a post per second. It's a bewildering rate of information; most Twitter users don't even use the concept of backlog, like in email.

Following some trusted tweet advisors, I installed Tweetdeck—sort of a *Bloomberg* [brokerage] for trading tweets. With this power tool and two large monitors, I was able to follow and keep up with a half dozen simultaneous conversations . . . all while monitoring email, Facebook and trying to get work done on the side. The effect is quite mesmerizing and I fell into a peak experience of social networking.

A few empirical observations about swimming in the deep end:

First, it's genuinely an addictive process. I used to design video games, so I'm pretty good at tuning gameplay "action.".... Twitter is definitely designed to encourage addictive usage. When I designed games, we would measure eyeblink rates to see if the player was entering a state of "flow" during gameplay. If the blink rate dropped precipitously after a few minutes of play, the game would most likely be a hit. And if you test a heavy twitter user in the same way, I'll bet that a similar thing is happening—a drop in the blink rate, some pupil dilation, and a surge in neuro-adrenaline.

Second, Twitter differs from regular chatrooms and instant messaging because it removes the idea of boundaries. In a chatroom, you can see that you're in a room titled "Golf in the Kingdom" and there are 25 people. So you can get a sense of the crowd and subject matter. In Twitter, no such virtual boundaries exist ... you're simply talking into the stream, and anyone at all might talk back. The more followers you have, the greater the likelihood that somebody's listening, but it's much more like CB radio than a cocktail party. You simply don't know who's listening or might reply ... and there are absolutely no moderators out there.

Third, on the Internet, you run into all sorts of interesting people. But on Twitter, you do it so much faster. Once I installed Tweetdeck, I only spent four hours twittering in high speed, but managed to interact with perhaps ten times the normal number of people I'd expect to run into via chatrooms. The innovation guru John Kao once told me that *serendipity is what makes innovation go faster* ... and often wished for a serendipity pedal that he could step on to increase random connections at companies. Twitter is serendipity on steroids.

I started my experiment tuning into the #haiku channel, @twitterhaiku wrote:

twitter followers. . .
from all over the planet. . .
how cool! hello, all!

Another entry, a bit more prosaic but reminiscent of the typical tweet, by @keithvassallo:

> *went to the movies. . .*
> *saw monsters vs aliens. . .*
> *nacho cheese was cold*

I contributed one:

> *I sit and twitter*
> *talking to everybody*
> *and nobody too*

This is cool. Kind of fun. Then I watched what was happening in #innovation. (Not much.) And then I chitchatted with people at random, as they flowed by. Eventually, I ran into a very intellectually stimulating woman named Alexa, and chatted with her while allowing myself to feel a little smitten for a bit. *Yeah, this is definitely entertaining.*

Twitter is significant because it amplifies whatever effect computer interactivity has on people.

Then I ran into a glitch. As a newbie, I had mixed up *reply* with *direct reply*. It's a Twitter *faux pas* equivalent to leaving the microphone on after a speech. A couple of kind souls explained what I was doing wrong and after clarifying the UI [user interface], I was able to turn off the mic. However, one power user—whose online persona is somewhat reminiscent of Meryl Streep's character in the film *Doubt*—decided to raise a virtual pitchfork and literally banish me from twitterland (known as a "suspension"). She was relentless, ignoring every apology and gesture of peace, and even stalked me on the web for a bit . . . a bit like someone who missed taking her meds.

For me, it was kind of exciting, "*Wow, my first hatetweet! I'm finally a celebrity!*"

But all joking aside, there are some power users out there who are deadly serious about their little corner of the twitter-verse, and emotional flareups can happen with just as much intensity as email flaming. This brings me to the primary thesis of this article, that Twitter is significant because it *amplifies* whatever effect computer interactivity has on people. . . . Twitter is the first *tweetch* game of social networking.

The Neurophysiology of Twitter

In fact, there's a neuroscientist saying that there is a neurophysiological basis for such concerns. The Baroness Susan Greenfield, professor of synaptic pharmacology at Lincoln College, Oxford, and director of the Royal Institution, recently testified to members of the British government that social network sites risk *"infantilising the mid-21st century mind, leaving it characterised by short attention spans, sensationalism, inability to empathise and a shaky sense of identity"*.

Greenfield told the House of Lords that social network sites are putting attention spans in jeopardy, warning: *"If the young brain is exposed from the outset to a world of fast action and reaction . . . such rapid interchange might accustom the brain to operate over such timescales. Perhaps when in the real world such responses are not immediately forthcoming, we will see such behaviours and call them attention-deficit disorder. It might be helpful to investigate whether the near total submersion of our culture in [such] technologies over the last decade might in some way be linked to the threefold increase over this period in prescriptions for methylphenidate, the drug prescribed for attention-deficit hyperactivity disorder."*

More importantly, Lady Greenfield also warned there is a risk of loss of empathy, which I believe is due to the fact that in cyber life, you can't see the subtle emotional cues on the faces of your victims as you send off that deliciously sarcastic email or get someone suspended for the hell of it. In linguistic theory, there are these rich facial and auditory gestures called *phatics*. It's the nod of the head or "uh huh" that tells the speaker that you're getting the message, it's clear-to-send, so keep it coming.

With face to face communications, the speaker is able to rely on the expression of the slightest note of distress on the listener's face, or even the silence on the phone, to realize that something he or she just said upset the listener. You know that silence. It's when your heart starts palpitating and you whine into your Bluetooth headset, *"Honey? Honey? Are you there? Are you mad at me?"*

That dance of rich metalinguistic feedback allows complex emotional communication to flow optimally, and without it, we end up with a worst case scenario for humanity that Lady Greenfield envisions. The real world of touch and phatics and eye gazing provides emotional richness that simply does not exist in the cyberworld.

In twenty years, we humans will adapt to handle what now looks like an indigestible volume of information without even breaking a sweat.

If the minds of our children are reinforced by too much twitter time and not enough running around in the backyard time, slowly trained to operate without metalinguistic nuances . . . is there a chance we'll raise a generation of kids with Asperger's syndrome? Are we inexorably marching toward a dystopian future, promising an ample supply of virtual flame-wars, limited empathy, borderline personalities, and who knows . . . maybe even the key ingredient for an entire series of Columbine massacres?

Now ask yourself, in order to see where Lady Greenfield is coming from, how much more emotionally limited can you be, than in a cyberverse limited to 140 characters?

Personally, I think that Lady Greenfield is overstating the risk. I think that the situation is similar to the development of freeways. Imagine transporting someone from the 1900s, and sticking them behind the wheel of a car today, speeding down the freeway. . . . Obviously, it would be a terrifying experience for our time traveler. Now, ask yourself, could someone in the 19th century even imagine a world where millions of teenagers happily drive down such freeways *while applying lipstick?*

The human brain is an amazingly adaptive system, and will surely be able to accommodate virtually any acceleration of information and scope of multi-tasking over time. In twenty years, we humans will adapt to handle what now looks like an indigestible volume of information without even breaking a sweat . . . you can bet on that, for sure.

The Twitter Singularity?

Perhaps Twitter is even part of our evolutionary process, like that initial adaptation we now call neuro-plasticity during that first evolutionary venture, during that first mutation of brain cells? For those who don't feel like looking it up on wikipedia, neuro-plasticity relates to how the brain learns, by adding or removing connections, or adding cells. Researchers have discovered that norepinephrine, a neuro-adrenaline dubbed "the stress hormone", increases brain plasticity. But that's kind of obvious . . . when your life's threatened, of course your brain is going to want to remember everything that's just about to happen.

Perhaps our brains, in a similar way, require stress and pressure to expand its capacities, and so we are now being pushed by new applications like Twitter to increase our base processing speeds—enabling a global network of brains that advance in lock step with the increasing speed of computer processors and search engines? Like the boundary-less Twitter-verse, where exactly *is* the boundary between our brains and the Internet?

Wow, big questions, huh? As for me, I'm leaning toward quitting the twitting. [Psychiatrist] R.D. Laing once said, "*Mys-*

tics and schizophrenics find themselves in the same ocean, but the mystics swim whereas the schizophrenics drown." The same could be said for the Internet and this river of human awareness. Twitter really *is* a significant time sink, and honestly, I'm more Zen than zap these days. I prefer to be the mystic reflecting quietly on my life and coming up with "My 25 List" on Facebook, than multitasking myself into a schizophrenic, shouting to everybody and nobody at the same time, listening to voices in the ether.

4

Twitter Has Played a Major Role in Political Change

Yigal Schleifer

Based in Washington, DC, Yigal Schleifer is a journalist covering Turkey and is the former Istanbul correspondent for the Christian Science Monitor.

The 2009 presidential election protests in Iran demonstrate that Twitter can play a role in driving political change and civil movements. Facing government crackdowns on social network sites and telecommunications, Iranians took to Twitter to distribute photos, organize protests, and report on the aftermath of the contested election. In fact, the messaging service was powerful in Iran because it is an open-ended application, which makes blocking the site extremely difficult. And as a social networking tool, Twitter brought Iran's struggles to a global stage, heightening awareness and solidarity. While experts state that Twitter cannot be credited with catalyzing the protests, it is a technology that can enable such movements.

Before Iran, there was Moldova, which had its own (unsuccessful) "Twitter Revolution" back in April [2009], when young activists used online tools to coordinate protests against the country's dubiously reelected Communist government. In Egypt, meanwhile, a new generation of activists has

Yigal Schleifer, "Why Iran's Twitter Revolution Is Unique," *Christian Science Monitor*, June 19, 2009. Copyright © 2012 by Yigal Schleifer. All rights reserved. Reproduced by permission.

come to embrace Facebook and Internet-based social networking applications to protest (again, mostly unsuccessfully) their repressive government.

But new-media experts say that Iran's civil resistance movement is unique because the government's tight control of media and the Internet has spawned a generation adept at circumventing cyber roadblocks, making the country ripe for a technology-driven protest movement.

"This is a country where you have tens of thousands of bloggers, and these bloggers have been in a situation where the Internet has been filtered since 2004. Anyone worth their salt knows how to find an open proxy [to get around government firewalls and filters], knows how to work around censorship," says Ethan Zuckerman, a research fellow at Harvard University's Berkman Center for Internet and Society in Cambridge, Mass. "The Iranian government, by filtering the Internet for so long, has actually trained a cadre of people who really know how to get around censorship."

As the government has cracked down on everything from cellphone service to Facebook, Twitter has emerged as the most powerful way to disseminate photos, organize protests, and describe street scenes in the aftermath of the contested June 12 [2009] election. Iranians' reliance on the social-networking tool has elevated it from a banal way to update one's friends in 140-character bursts to an agent for historic changes in the Islamic Republic.

Only North Korea, Eritrea, and Turkmenistan Do Worse

Iran exercises strict control of both the Internet and the mainstream media. In its 2007 World Press Freedom Index, Reporters Without Borders ranked the country 166th of 169 countries, worse than authoritarian regimes such as Burma and Cuba, and only better than Turkmenistan, North Korea, and Eritrea.

And while 35 percent of Iranians use the Internet—considerably higher than the Middle East average of 26 percent—the Iranian government operates what has been described as one of the most extensive filtering systems in the world.

"Thinking that technology can only help pro-democracy protestors is naïve," says Evgeny Morozov, a fellow at the Open Society Institute studying the impact of new media in authoritarian states. "Are [Iranian President Mahmoud] Ahmedinejad's supporters using technology to also mobilize? I'm sure of that."

> *Some experts . . . warn about overstating the role that new media and technology can play in organizing a successful protest movement.*

Hamid Tehrani of Global Voices Online, a website that aggregates the work of bloggers from around the world, says Iranian officials may have contributed to rising power of social networking tools by temporarily lifting some of the filtering restrictions on them in recent months, apparently in an effort to put on a friendly and democratic face in the run up to the elections.

"Facebook, YouTube and blogs were very important during the election campaign," says Mr. Tehrani, the Brussels-based Iran editor for Global Voices.

"Maybe they didn't forecast the consequences of easing up on the social networking applications. Now people have a very strong platform. They got used to using these tools."

Technology Is Only a Tool—the Strategy Is What Matters

Some experts, though, warn about overstating the role that new media and technology can play in organizing a successful protest movement.

In the Molodovan case, although Twitter and other new-media technologies might have helped in organizing protests against the country's rulers, the movement fizzled quickly. On the other hand, although the successful 2004 Orange Revolution was helped along by the use of the Internet and mobile phone text messaging, a Berkman Center study found that: "the Orange Revolution was largely made possible by savvy activists and journalists willing to take risks to improve their country."

"You have to be careful about not being too enamored about technology," says Peter Ackerman, founding chair of the International Center on Nonviolent Conflict in Washington. "It's sexy and it's fun and we can relate to it, but unless there's a strategy for creating loyalty shifts to the other side . . . and a set of goals everyone can unify around, you're not going to get to where you need to be."

But while he cautions that it would be incorrect to credit Twitter and other new media with sparking the mass protests in Iran, Ackerman does see them as playing an enabling role to a movement that he says could ultimately be successful—particularly as it moves outside Tehran.

[Twitter is] far more naturally censorship resistant than most other Web sites.

Why Is Twitter So Powerful? It's "Half-Baked"

As Iran approaches the one-week mark of election, the Iranian authorities seem intent on reasserting their control over the Internet. Iran's Revolutionary Guard on Wednesday warned that anyone using sites such as Twitter for political purposes would be subject to retribution.

"We warn those who propagate riots and spread rumors that our legal action against them will cost them dearly," a statement from the military force on Wednesday said.

But technology experts say that completely blocking Twitter, whose open-ended design allows for its messages to be broadcast from various sources, will be very difficult.

"The very fact that Twitter itself is half-baked, coupled with its designers' willingness to let anyone build on top of it to finish baking it . . . is what makes it so powerful," Jonathan Zittrain, Professor of Law at Harvard Law School and faculty co-director of the Berkman Center, recently wrote on his blog.

"And with so many ways to get those tweets there and back without the user needing twitter.com, it's far more naturally censorship resistant than most other Web sites. Less really is more."

Globalizing a Local Struggle

Mr. Zuckerman of the Berkman Center says the value of Twitter and social networking tools may be to push a domestic agenda onto the world stage.

"I think social media at this point is most useful at making that what is a local struggle become a global struggle. I think that is what is happening here," he says.

"It is helping people globally feel solidarity and it's keeping international attention on what's happening. It's giving people a sense of involvement that they otherwise wouldn't have, and I think that's very important."

With Internet access in Iran now sometimes so slow and unreliable—due to a combination of heavy usage and government interference—as to be almost useless, Tehrani—the Global Voices editor—says Iranians may ultimately have to fall back on older technologies to do their organizing.

"In the end, I think the most important thing is like what happened in the 1979 revolution: person-to-person communication," he says.

5

The Role of Twitter in Political Change Is Exaggerated

Matthew Shaer

Matthew Shaer is a regular contributer to New York Magazine *and a former staff reporter at the* Christian Science Monitor.

The American media hailed the 2009 presidential election protests in Iran as the "Twitter Revolution," in which Iranians under authoritarian government control used the site to organize and publicize the protests. However, the view that the messaging service played such an important role is a skewed, inaccurate assessment of how events unfolded and lacks understanding of the nation's society and culture. For instance, updates and dispatches streaming from Iran were sent by the most frequent Twitter users—young people with pro-Western biases—who represent a very small, atypical segment of the population and had no viable connection to the mass demonstrations. Moreover, the protests were carefully orchestrated, while Twitter itself is not suited for mobilizing protests, since it serves as a source of intelligence on the revolutionaries' actions for the Iranian regime. This downside to the Twitter Revolution, however, was largely ignored and gave rise to ineffective Internet activism.

In today's *Boston Phoenix*, media critic Adam Reilly offers a typically sober analysis of Twitter's role in post-election Iran. His take: the social network allowed outsiders a view

Matthew Shaer, "Second guessing Twitter's effect on post-election Iran," *Christian Science Monitor*, June 25, 2009. Copyright © 2009 by Matthew Shaer. All rights reserved. Reproduced by permission.

into the turmoil on the streets of Tehran. Even more important, it allowed Americans to discuss, vet, filter, and label news that might otherwise have gone unread.

But Reilly—like an assortment of like-minded media critics—is skeptical that anything conclusive can be said about Twitter's direct effect on the protests. First, Reilly argues that Twitter has played such a "vital newsgathering role" mostly because many veteran journalists were either constrained by the Iranian government or forced to leave Iran. In a situation less punishing—say the ongoing Mark Sanford debacle—Twitter probably wouldn't have as much clout. The reason: trained reporters would still be able to function in a traditional manner.

Reilly also cautions against reading into Twitter as a populist tool. After all, couldn't Twitter just as easily be co-opted by the forces of the state? "Even if Twitter's role in the Iranian protest movement proves to have been as robust as some contend," Reilly writes:

> [T]hat won't mean that, as a technology, it's possessed of some sort of inherent, neo-Hegelian, collective-consciousness-manifesting benevolence. Just think, for example, how queasily handy Twitter would have been when the Hutus whipped up paranoid resentment of the Tutsis prior to the Rwandan genocide—or how similarly useful it could be for tech-savvy anti-Semites looking to organize a pogrom.

Parsing the Meaning of Another "Twitter Revolution"

This last idea is not without precedent. Writing on *The New Republic's* blog, Jason Zengerle last week pointed to an On the Media interview with Ethan Zuckerman, a fellow at Harvard's Berkman Center for Internet and Society. In the interview, Zuckerman discusses the "Twitter Revolution" in Moldova—

several days of postelection protest purportedly spurred on by the Twittering classes—but spends more time questioning Twitter's ultimate efficacy.

"My take on it at this point is that Twitter probably wasn't all that important in organizing the demonstration," Zuckerman said. "Where I think they were enormously important is helping people, particularly people in the Moldovan Diaspora, keep up with the events in real time." He pointed to the large Moldovan diaspora, and said that much of the Twittering had been recycled among Moldovans abroad.

"Roughly a quarter of all of the messages posted on Tuesday, the day of the actual demonstrations, were what we call re-tweets," Zuckerman said, adding that, "By Wednesday, a lot of what seems to be going on in the Twittering is a sort of self-congratulatory, hey, we just held a revolution over Twitter—isn't this exciting? Twitter will change the world."

Users can communicate information quickly and clearly [and] . . . they can reach a much wider audience than with a simple Facebook profile update.

Zuckerman then suggested that Twitter may have been incorporated by pro-government forces. "Fascinatingly," he said, "it looks like it is being used as a disinformation channel by forces who might have been aligned with the government, essentially trying to scare people away from demonstrating again."

In Our Pages

The *[Christian Science] Monitor* has written extensively on the "Twitter Revolution." On June 19, Yigal Schleifer wrote, "Twitter has emerged as the most powerful way to disseminate photos, organize protests, and describe street scenes in the aftermath of the contested June 12 election. Iranians' reliance on the social-networking tool has elevated it from a banal way to update one's friends in 140-character bursts to an agent for historic changes in the Islamic Republic."

And on June 17, I argued that [it is] the "terse, frenetic nature of the site that makes it so useful. Users can communicate information quickly and clearly, and with minimal effort. More important, they can reach a much wider audience than with a simple Facebook profile update." In that article, I pointed to a quote from social media guru Gaurav Mishra, who argued that the idea of a Twitter revolution was "suspect. . . . The amount of people who use these tools in Iran is very small and could not support protests that size," Mishra said.

For his part, Reilly writes that there is one easy way for us to figure out how Twitter impacted the events in Iran. "It's true that Twitter may have saved tens of thousands of lives in the days following the election," he acknowledges:

> Then again, it may not have saved any at all. We simply don't know, since no journalist or historian or political scientist has yet had the luxury of talking with key figures from the opposition and figuring out how important Twitter was in terms of protecting dissenters. No one's been able to study—with the precision required to make the sort of declaratory statement everyone currently craves—exactly what role Twitter played in mobilizing and sustaining resistance to the regime.

6

Twitter Has Transformed News and Reporting

Janic Tremblay

Janic Tremblay is a reporter at Radio-Canada, a French language Canadian public broadcaster.

Though it does not replace traditional media outlets, Twitter can be a source of news and a valuable tool for journalism. A recent experiment with five secluded journalists permitted to rely only on updates from Twitter and Facebook to stay informed—banning feeds from news organizations—revealed that the messaging service can be used to find or share information on current events. For instance, journalists can use tweets to search for and make contact with individuals involved in newsworthy stories for interviews and tweet their own stories to reach a wider number of readers. Nonetheless, the experiment also demonstrates that Twitter can be filled with speculations and inaccuracies and lacks in-depth news analysis. Journalists can no longer ignore Twitter and should learn to use it without compromising their own work.

*I*n February, five journalists from French-speaking public radio stations isolated themselves in a farmhouse in southern France to conduct an experiment. For five days they would stay informed by using only their social networks. Their ground rules forbid them to follow the feeds and tweets of any news media; to be informed, they had to rely solely on the tweets or Facebook

Janic Tremblay, "Twitter: Can It Be a Reliable Source of News?" *The Nieman Reports*, Summer 2010. Copyright © 2010 by The Nieman Reports. All rights reserved. Reproduced by permission.

*offerings of individuals or organizations such as nonprofits, gov-
ernment agencies, or educational institutions. One of the secluded journalists was reporter Janic Tremblay, who works at
Radio-Canada. In this article, he describes the experience and
the lessons he brought back to his work.*

"News will find you wherever you are." That's what a lot
of people think now that the Internet is in its third revolution—as the always on, always available Web. Thanks to Facebook, Twitter and the smartphone, we expect that we will be
informed in real time on just about any topic. We depend on
family members, close friends, and those who are part of our
digital networks to act as reporters, alerting us when something they feel is important has happened or is happening.
Within our chosen digital community, we are always connected, always informed. At least, that's how the story goes.

But is this how it actually happens? What kinds of information emerge through social networks? What do people talk
about after traditional news media sources have been removed?
Which news do they tweet? Or retweet? And do social networks help us find valuable information?

---

*Like all social media networks, the Twitter experience is
determined by those whose tweets we welcome into our
digital feed.*

We humbly set out with these questions—and others—in
mind, hoping we'd find a way to measure, though not in any
scientific way, the value our social networks held for us as
journalists. We set some rules, locked the door of our home in
Saint-Cyprien, and turned our full attention to the Web. From
there, many lessons—most discovered through Twitter—
flowed my way.

Twitter can be like radar: On our first night in France, I
went online and came across tweets from a man who had
been arrested during a demonstration in Moscow earlier that

day. He had been jailed for many hours and was tweeting about what was happening. I did not know him. Clearly we lived in different universes, but it turned out that a member of his social network is also part of mine. When my social networking friend retweeted his posts, he showed up in my Twitter feed, and there we were—connected, with me in a French farmhouse and he in jail in Moscow. And so I tweeted him directly, then later contacted him by phone. He spoke French very well, an important detail for a French-speaking radio reporter. He told me about his arrest and the condition of his detention, and so I had a good story. With the traditional tools of journalists, the odds of me finding this man would have been close to zero. However, I believe situations like this one happen rarely, as best I can tell from my experience and that of my colleagues.

Twitter can steer off course: It was the third night of our stay in Saint-Cyprien. Apparently a very loud noise had been heard in the city of Lille in northern France. Lots of tweets talked about this noise. It was obvious that people were trying to figure out what had happened as this topic became the talk of the French Twitter-sphere that night. Many hypotheses were tweeted; it was an explosion, a fire, or maybe a nuclear problem. In the next day's newspaper (which I could not read at the time), a reporter unraveled the mystery with a story of what actually happened. The loud sound was from an airplane that had crossed the sound barrier over the city. On Twitter, I had not seen anyone come up with this explanation. So while we knew what was being talked about via the tweets, we had no idea what was happening.

What I like about you is me: Like all social media networks, the Twitter experience is determined by those whose tweets we welcome into our digital feed. And digital communities tend to congregate around interests or issues. This isn't so very different from how audiences flock to various news media (Fox News or CNN, for example) based on the topics or perspective they are fairly certain they'll find there. It can feel reassuring to follow like-minded people. Who doesn't like to have their opinions confirmed? Yet choosing such a specific path to news can also be limiting since it can be hard to count on friends to broaden our horizons. Like a couple who thinks alike, neither brings much new to their conversation or thinking.

> *One lesson I took from this experience is that what interests the public . . . is not the same as the public interest, at least as journalists conceive of it.*

Tweeting Lessons

As I think back on these five days—and what I learned, I focus on the social networks I brought with me into our house. This experience taught me that they were not diversified enough. News reached me, but in my mix of tweets I could find little in-depth analysis or many international news reports. Nor did I find much discussion about news taking place among members of my network. And only very rarely did I hear much about economic news.

I came to understand that there is a science to this quest for creating the right network. It's an empirical process, one that requires lots of time and thought and effort. And the search for the best sources of news never ends. I also concluded from this experience that finding symphonic notes amid all the noise of these networks is not easy. Moreover, on Twitter, people tend to tweet what they have picked up from the traditional news media; what they add is an introduction to what they've found, letting their friends or followers know that they found it interesting or new, moving or fascinating. Right now how this exchange of information happens is very tied in with the tools of social media that we have available to us, and this is something else we experienced firsthand during our week in France.

One lesson I took from this experience is that what interests the public—as I saw interest expressed by what they share and highlight through these social media networks—is not the same as the public interest, at least as journalists conceive of it. Of course, these two ideas might grow closer in time as Twitter becomes more popular.

When only a few journalists tweet—and do so constantly—they occupy a lot of the space. This means that their perspective on the news could become the dominant (or possibly the only) interpretation of an event.

Getting Personal

While in the farmhouse, I managed to gather almost all of the important news during the more than 60 hours that I spent on Twitter. (After we emerged, I checked to see what stories I might have missed.) Retweets turned out to be essential for my newsgathering since I was not allowed to follow any media organizations. But being constrained, as I was, helped me realize how often messages that journalists send out are retweeted. On the other hand, the stories sent out by newspapers and broadcast entities didn't get retweeted too much. What this told me is that there is a strong tug of personal engagement within the digital community, evidenced as members of the community retweet stories that are brought to the Twitter feed by an author or journalist himself.

At CBC/Radio-Canada where I work, very few journalists use Twitter. Even so our news organization has a Twitter account with more than 30,000 followers. However, during the five days of the experiment, I did not find any news from Radio-Canada. The reason: no retweets. A popular French-

Canadian newspaper, La Presse, also has a Twitter account with just about the same number of followers, and I did not get any retweets from La Presse's feed, either. But many journalists at La Presse tweet personally, so many of their stories made their way to me through retweets.

The lesson is simple: journalists should tweet about their stories. By doing so, they might get a higher penetration rate of clicking on links and sharing among followers; they will also likely gather new followers through this retweeting, and ultimately getting the news out will inform more people, which is our goal.

But there are other key considerations about why more journalists tweeting is better than fewer. When only a few journalists tweet—and do so constantly—they occupy a lot of the space. This means that their perspective on the news could become the dominant (or possibly the only) interpretation of an event and, if this happens, the lack of diversity of the information becomes an important issue.

Social Media and Journalism

While social media networks can be a personalized resource for news, it is virtually impossible to work eight hours a day, take care of the kids, regularly ride the train to work and back, read books and articles, follow what hundreds of people are tweeting at the same time, and click on the links they suggest and end up absorbing anything fully. Even with a deliberate focus on doing so, as we had for those five days in the absence of any distractions, this was hard.

This is one reason why I so firmly believe that traditional news media outlets are still essential—as the people who can provide reliable journalistic content, which then forms the backbone of Twitter's links. This is not to say that any others who can bring additional knowledge and information into the mix shouldn't do so. They should, but having this foundation built by the practitioners of journalism's standards and ethics is vital.

Still, it now is not possible for journalists to ignore or neglect Twitter. Too much is happening there. Every individual journalist—along with every news organization—should put strategies in place to determine the best ways to do our work in tandem with the culture and habits of social media networks. Also, figuring out how best to thrive in the Twitter environment without compromising our work as journalists (and not as advocates) is part of what the job entails today. Tweets are easily sent and they leave traces for a long time— just as all words and pictures do in this digital territory. When personal opinion reigns supreme—with a side taken and a perception settling in—then serving the public interest as a journalist just got harder to do.

7

Twitter Should Not Be Used for News and Reporting

Melissa Hart

Melissa Hart teaches travel and feature writing at the School of Journalism and Communication at the University of Oregon; she also teaches memoir courses for the online extension program at the University of California, Berkeley.

Reporting the news on the microblogging service Twitter—as bits of information in 140 characters or less—may quickly offer basic facts and premises, but it does not make a news story. Twittering does not compare to the investigation and analysis that goes into well-crafted journalism, in which the reporter pays full attention to the subject and surroundings, capturing immersive details to share with readers. While the service is useful for finding sources and providing informative news links, it is thoroughly reported, provocative investigative pieces that challenge readers, not one-sentence tweets from laptops and phones.

Just before the start of spring term, a friend and colleague in journalism sent an e-mail message to our department: Technology had changed, she wrote; perhaps our reporting curriculum should change with it. She planned to teach with a focus on live blogging and Twitter, and suggested that those students not particularly interested in using the new technology should be tracked into the other reporting class.

Melissa Hart, "The Trouble With Twitter," *Chronicle of Higher Education*, vol 55, no 42, July 27, 2009. Copyright © 2009 by Melissa Hart. All rights reserved. Reproduced by permission.

That is, my reporting class—one in which we emphatically would not use Twitter.

For those not in the know, Twitter is a microblogging service that allows members to report on what they're seeing, thinking, and feeling by posting comments that are limited to just 140 characters each. You can subscribe to someone's Twitter feed and receive what are called "tweets"—brief bits of information like "Sat through another of Prof. Hart's interminable lectures on the glories of literary nonfiction."

With its laughable name that itself suggests foolishness, Twitter has become the butt of media jokes. Doonesbury's Garry Trudeau created several comic strips mocking the inherent narcissism of its users and its inadequacy as a reporting tool. Earlier this year, Slate offered up a mockumentary of a start-up "nanoblogging" company called Flutter that allows users only 40 characters. "It just takes too long to compose a message with 140 characters," one entrepreneur says on the film, "and then you start getting bombarded by a few tweets, and it's like hundreds of characters that you have to read."

Not everyone is laughing, though.

News, but Not a News Story

A few months ago, I sat across a cafe table from a local newspaper editor and watched the bewilderment on his face as he told me how the Internet has altered print journalism at his own paper. Recently some of its readers complained when they heard through word of mouth about a car accident in town but couldn't find updates on the newspaper's Web site. "We told them they had to wait until we'd investigated and could post a full report," he said, "and they demanded to know why we couldn't just Twitter the information right then." The answer, of course, is that 140 characters gives reporters just enough room to note who, what, where, why, and how in the most basic terms. That may be news, but it's not a news story.

"We're talking about laying people off," the editor added, "but hiring a full-time Internet reporter. And that person will Twitter."

On Twitter, the notes become the story, devoid of even five minutes of reflection on the writer's way to the computer.

With this new form of journalism to consider, I attended a lecture on "The Incredible Shrinking Newsroom" given by Martin Baron, editor of *The Boston Globe*. I sat sandwiched between two journalism students, both of them busily texting from their cellphones. In front of me sat another young man, bent over his laptop. I looked around and spotted even more students hunched over computers, wielding cellphones, or ready with their BlackBerrys, thumbs poised, waiting for Baron to begin his lecture. (They reminded me of a science teacher I had in high school, a man who told his students with some delight that humans were destined to evolve into an egg shape with one finger.)

The wistful editor noted how, in January 2007, he was forced to shut down all of the *Globe's* foreign bureaus because of declining revenue. Did the busily typing students, staring at their screens, hear the sorrow in Baron's voice as he recounted those closings, calling them "a signal of diminished ambitions"? Did those students notice the pain, fear, and indignation on the faces of their fellow audience members—older community members who had biked across town to hear the lecture, as well as 21-year-olds poised to graduate with dreams of careers in newspaper journalism? Or were they too busy Twittering?

Already, I can imagine some of my more technologically savvy friends chastising me—"Oh, Melissa, you're such an essayist." It's true: I tend to sit on a subject for a while, ruminating on it before disseminating my perspective. "You're like a cow chewing its cud," a friend once told me. "Reporters just take notes, then write the story."

To those who Twitter, the reporter who investigates a story before offering it to the public must also seem tediously ruminant. On Twitter, the notes become the story, devoid of even five minutes of reflection on the writer's way to the computer. I can see that there are times—an airplane landing in the Hudson, a presidential election in Iran—when this type of impromptu journalism becomes a necessity, and an exciting one at that. Luckily, reporters still exist to make sense of information bytes and expand upon them for readers—but for how much longer?

I worry that microblogging cheats my students out of their trump card: a mindful attention to the subject in front of them, so that they can capture its sights and sounds, its smells and tactile qualities, to share with readers. How can Twittering stories from laptops and phones possibly replace the attentive journalist who tucks a digital recorder artfully under a notepad, pencil behind one ear, and gives full attention to the subject at hand?

What is news? Is it a stark factual sentence, or a well-crafted story steeped in sensory details, heavily dependent on the reporter's presence at the scene?

A Ridiculous Method for Reporting the News

After Baron's lecture, I read the students' tweets. They commented on Baron's backward-looking pessimism; they noted the irony of the *Globe*'s thriving Web site. Good, useful information—but with a lot of gaps. No one noted how the editor stood small at the podium, as if defeated, delivering what was supposed to be a rousing call to action in a voice diminished by desperation—the reason being, we found out later, the

New York Times Company's threats that morning to shut down the *Globe* unless pay cuts went into effect immediately.

I read several tweets that focused on Baron's advice to "tell revealing stories in new ways and with dazzling new tools"— but none that described the audience, none that included observations about the hopeful young reporters who read their fate in the accounts of disappearing daily newspapers. There were no posts about the elderly man who stood up at the microphone after Baron's lecture to argue fiercely for the viability of tangible news.

I went home after the lecture and—hypocritically, I admit—updated my Facebook status and my blog to declare how much I despise Twitter. My friend in the journalism department responded by forwarding me an e-mail message she'd sent to her reporting class, showing how Twitter serves as a source of links to longer news stories. I found myself conceding this unexpected usefulness for microblogging as a source for links to complete *New York Times* articles on art and films, and as a venue for alerts from Powell's Books regarding upcoming sales.

Still, as a method for reporting the news, Twitter strikes me as ridiculous. It begs the question: What is news? Is it a stark factual sentence, or a well-crafted story steeped in sensory details, heavily dependent on the reporter's presence at the scene?

Arguing the latter, I sent my reporting students out to complete a digital-photo scavenger hunt on their beat—a three-block radius in Springfield, Ore. I instructed them to take public transportation, then find and photograph a list of 20 signs, shops, and landmarks. They were also to interview two strangers and ask them what they liked and disliked about their community. In this way, the students would learn first-hand about a new place and its people in order to produce engaging, thoroughly reported articles.

I worried that they'd find the assignment silly, irrelevant in this technological age. But no one countered my scavenger hunt with, "Can't we just research the community on the Internet?" Instead, with surprising good will on a rainy morning, the students set off in pairs to photograph rabbit carcasses hanging in a butcher shop, murals, graffiti, and witty signage in front of the new, controversial strip club. They interviewed strangers and reported back to me as we headed back an hour later to sit around a table in a classroom sans computers.

"I'm going back to the butcher shop to interview the owner," one young man told us, his eyes glowing. "Besides rabbit, he sells rattlesnake and alligator meat. Who buys that stuff?" Another student decided to devote the term to immersion journalism, inspired by a sign he'd seen outside a local strip club that day: "It said, 'We've got your stimulus package right here,'" he told us. "I want to investigate why these clubs thrive financially in the middle of a recession." The group continued to discuss their story ideas, and I left class that day excited to read their feature articles and profiles, reported by students eager to immerse themselves in learning about butcher shops and gun stores and diners.

A Path from Question to Revelation

If it's true that writers read in the genres they most enjoy crafting, then give me a painstakingly crafted investigative piece any day—a provocative story that challenges the reader to accompany the reporter on a path from question to revelation. Give me *The Boston Globe*'s Michael Paulson and his incisive coverage of the election of the first openly gay bishop in the Episcopal Church. Give me Sonia Nazario's heartbreaking series on a Honduran boy's illegal journey to the United States, printed in the *Los Angeles Times*.

Likely I'm being woefully short-sighted in my response to reporting via Twitter. Perhaps a news article really can be crafted, haikulike, in 140 characters.

My hat is off to those who can do it. I just don't want to read it.

8

Twitter May Become Profitable

Knowledge@Wharton

Knowledge@Wharton is the online business journal of the Wharton School at the University of Pennsylvania.

Twitter's "Promoted Tweets," in which advertising messages reach users based on their searches, is its first major attempt to become profitable. Experts have differing views on whether this or other potential strategies, such as charging for longer tweets and setting in place pricing models for businesses, will successfully monetize the microblogging service. Additionally, there is disagreement about whether companies view Twitter as an essential marketing tool that is worth the investment. Still, major businesses are continuing to use the service to reach and engage customers, who may be more open to promotions and sales pitches than other social network users.

It was a tweet like many others from Starbucks, promising free refills to customers who brought in reusable tumblers on Earth Day [in 2010].

But the message came to users in a different way—it appeared at the top of Twitter search results pages, even for those who weren't among the coffee giant's followers. And there was a tiny tag in the corner of the update, outlined in yellow and reading "Promoted by Starbucks Coffee."

"Can Twitter Promote Itself Into Profitability?", *Knowledge@Wharton*, May 26, 2012. Copyright © 2012 Knowledge@Wharton. All rights reserved. Used by permission and protected by the Copyright Laws of the United States. The printing, copying, redistribution, or retransmission of this Content without express written permission is prohibited.

The ubiquitous Seattle-based chain is one of the first guinea pigs in an effort by Twitter to generate revenue from the micro-blogging service. The new ad system was unveiled last month with five participating companies, including Best Buy electronics stores, the Red Bull soft drink company, Sony Pictures, Starbucks, airline Virgin America and the Bravo TV network. Twitter Chief Operating Officer Dick Costolo recently told Reuters that the San Francisco-based company hopes to add hundreds of new "Promoted Tweet" partners into the mix by the fourth quarter of 2010.

"We're going to live in a world where we need to be generating hundreds of millions of dollars in revenue," Costolo told Reuters. "We're thinking about big, big numbers."

Twitter's user ranks include high profile names that run the gamut from Paula Abdul to Lance Armstrong. The company's value was put at $1 billion last year. But Twitter has yet to generate a profit. Wharton experts and others— some of whom tweet and others of whom don't—say finding a successful model for the Promoted Tweet is only one of the challenges the company must overcome to avoid the fate of former "next big things" like Netscape, Excite or Pets.com.

It is a question of whether Twitter will, in the long run, be something mainstream America deems necessary, which will determine its business value.

Twitter's Business Conundrums

The company's set of business conundrums are intertwined. How can it help businesses create a level of engagement with consumers that turns the service—which allows users to communicate in bites of 140 characters or fewer—into a useful tool for marketing and customer service? And how can Twitter then parlay those efforts into a viable, income-producing strategy?

Twitter has had plenty of success at gaining public exposure. According to an Edison Research/Arbitron study conducted in February, 87% of Americans 12 and older know what Twitter is—about the same number as those who were aware of Facebook. But while 41% of that group actively used Facebook, only 7% were actually sending updates to Twitter.

"Seventeen million people [use Twitter], which is nothing to sneeze at," says Tom Webster, Edison Research's vice president of strategy and marketing, who oversaw the survey. "Businesses are certainly using it as part of an overall marketing strategy, at least for now. It is a question of whether Twitter will, in the long run, be something mainstream America deems necessary, which will determine its business value."

Twitter began as part of a brainstorming session at the small San Francisco podcasting company Odeo, in March 2006. The company's principals saw that the podcast business was being usurped by bigger companies like Apple and wanted to find a new product on which to concentrate. The idea that came to the fore was a way for someone to send short messages to tell small groups of friends or contacts what he or she was doing at a given time. Twitter limited itself to 140 Short Message Service (SMS) characters and initially was used for communication among Odeo employees and friends before launching to the public in July 2006.

Twitter made its biggest initial splash at the South by Southwest music and interactive media festival in March 2007, when it placed plasma screens in the hallways of the conference venues to display the tweets attendees were sending about their activities. Conference speakers mentioned it, bloggers enthused over it, and the service ultimately won the festival's Web award. Twitter then began to grow more quickly, with the company reporting 500,000 tweets per quarter in 2007 and then 100 million per quarter the next year. For the first quarter of 2010, the company reported that more than four billion tweets were sent using the service.

"The real challenge, though, is how Twitter is going to monetize this. It is not obvious at the moment," says Eric Bradlow, a Wharton marketing professor and co-director of Wharton Interactive Media Initiative (WIMI), noting that the trick for Internet businesses has been implementing money-making modifications without alienating, and losing, users. "Maybe they can start charging for longer tweets or start putting in a two-tier pricing model for businesses. Maybe they can have some charge after a certain number of tweets or they can have advertising somewhere on the Twitter page or in tweets themselves."

Opinion is mixed among experts about whether Promoted Tweets—or, to be sure, anything else—will be the way to transform Twitter into a profitable business.

Turning Tweets into Dollar Signs

The Promoted Tweet is just that—an advertising message that appears on the top of the results screen in response to a user's search. In Starbucks' case, for example, anyone looking for updates containing the word "coffee" might see Promoted Tweets from the company. Companies pay Twitter to run the ads, which look and function like any other tweet (for example, users can send reply comments) except for a "promoted by" tag in one corner.

Twitter executives have been careful to say the Promoted Tweets model is only in the experimental phase. Earlier this week [in May 2010], however, the company announced that it was banning third-party advertisements from the site, a move observers think is part of an effort to gain control over monetization of the service. Opinion is mixed among experts about whether Promoted Tweets—or, to be sure, anything else—will be the way to transform Twitter into a profitable business. "I think Promoted Tweets are a bad idea," says Wharton marketing professor and WIMI co-director Peter Fader. "It's one thing to have a relatively unobtrusive display ad above or next to a set of search results on a monitor, but this will really ruin the user experience on Twitter."

Fader thinks Twitter ought to start looking for a different route to financial success: "The right business model for Twitter is to be bought by another company and have the user experience folded into a broader array of media services. I see little advantage to Twitter as a stand-alone entity."

But Kartik Hosanagar, Wharton professor of operations and information management, believes patience is the best policy for those dismissing Twitter right now. "Promoted Tweets are the first major monetization initiative Twitter has announced," Hosanagar notes. "Just as Google is successful with search ads because it is exceedingly good at matching results with user intentions, Twitter will need to be effective at providing Promoted Tweets that users find useful. They need and intend to do much more than just match keywords."

Twitter has other monetization possibilities, Hosanagar says, but "the challenge is that it is still growing and it does not want to lock itself into . . . a strategy that might interfere with that growth. . . . For example, Twitter made several million dollars with deals to allow major search engines like Google and Bing to index [the site's] data flows in real time," he adds. "I have no doubt that Twitter can generate more revenue. The question is just how big an opportunity it has."

Still, Fader warns that Twitter suffers from the very frivolity that generates a lot of the service's publicity. The biggest buzz from the site comes from the mini-scandals and sound bites that arise from its use by celebrities—and that might make it more difficult for businesses and consumers to take the service seriously as an entrepreneurial tool.

"That people were tuning into CNN to see how many followers Ashton Kutcher got, [garnered] Twitter a whole lot of publicity, but in the long run probably didn't do it any good,"

Fader says. "More serious people might say, 'I won't be using that.' . . . It is a shame that it is saddled with this cutesy name and a bird for a logo and the race between Ashton and Britney Spears for millions of followers. It would almost be better to split off the entertainment aspect into a different service [because Twitter] really does have an opportunity to have real business and consumer uses."

Twitter has put some effort into showing businesses how the site can work for them.

The Wild West of Social Media

But Vivek Wahdwa, the director of research at Duke University's Center for Entrepreneurship and Research Commercialization, says the more light-hearted aspects of Twitter don't count it out of the business realm, especially in the area of Promoted Tweets. "I found there are two types of Twitter users: those who tweet every time they go to the bathroom, and those who have intelligent things to say," notes Wahdwa, who was originally a Twitter skeptic, but now uses it for professional communications and thinks it is useful when employed in tandem with other social media services. "You can judge by the tweets of both groups what their general interests are—like Google does with web searches—and target messages to them. I can see [Promoted Tweets] as an opportunity for Twitter [the way that] search ads are for Google."

And Twitter has put some effort into showing businesses how the site can work for them. The company created a page on its website to offer suggestions for "tweet-based" marketing and customer service campaigns. For example, an employee of the New York-based ice cream chain Tasti D-Lite uses the company's Twitter feed to answer customer questions and take suggestions. In another example, the Dell computer store posts coupons and special offers for electronics that are exclusive to Twitter.

But "by no means does [Twitter] have a monopoly," on companies' social media strategies, warns Fader. "LinkedIn and Facebook are trying things. Someone will figure it out. To have microblogs with other features out there seems an inevitable way for businesses to market. It is the Wild West out there right now with all these methods of communication."

Engaging the "Lurkers"

Dell and Tasti D-Lite are examples of businesses that found a way to engage customers using Twitter. But experts question if companies will ever be able to reach broader audiences that way—and if the answer is no, how can Twitter keep itself on the "must" list for investment in social media and Internet marketing?

The Edison Research/Arbitron survey found that the majority of Twitter users are "lurkers," or those who follow various people, but don't take part in conversations on the service or contribute a significant amount of original tweets. "Twitter appears to be functioning as more of a broadcast medium [as] compared to Facebook and many other social networking sites and services," according to the report. Because of that, Twitter users might be more susceptible to sales pitches: "The percentage of Twitter users who follow brands is more than three times higher than similar behavior expressed by social networking users in general. Significant percentages of regular Twitter users report using the service not only to seek opinions about companies, products and services, but to provide those opinions as well."

Ultimately, then, says Wharton legal studies and business ethics professor Andrea M. Matwyshyn, Twitter's penetration and success in its business applications will be whether those "lurkers" become really interested customers for the businesses who seek them. "Some uses of social networks, like Twitter, can be merely a time-killing mechanism if you are trapped in a waiting room," she says. "Now with BlackBerries and other mobile devices, there is no time or space barrier to communications. But that doesn't mean it's a necessity for the customer either. Do I really want to know about the new Coke product at any moment? It isn't certain yet, so we'll just have to wait to see how it shakes out."

9

Twitter May Not Become Profitable

Joe Hagan

Joe Hagan is a contributing editor at New York Magazine, Rolling Stone, *and* Men's Journal.

Twitter is aiming to turn its 140-character tweets into a profitable advertising model and business, but it struggles with fundamental questions about the company and its audience. Rather than a social network, Twitter is akin to a broadcasting service that connects audiences to talent—with ads that must remain unobtrusive to the experience. But its structure, audience, talent, or advertisers are not as developed as needed. While efficiently organizing its two hundred million daily tweets would make content easier to aggregate, the free-form quality that defines Twitter would be lost. Also, ad-sponsored tweets—in which ads are smoothly inserted into the updates of highly followed celebrities and public figures on Twitter—are still far from reality. Whether the company and its engineers can rise to these challenges and meet expectations before Twitter's popularity fades remains to be seen.

OHHH MY GOD—A BIG JIANT SPIDER JUST CRAWLED ON MY PILLOW!!!!!! ARGHHHH OMG OMG OMG EWWWW OMG!!!!!!!!!!!!

The tweet from Meghan McCain, the 27-year-old daughter of the senator from Arizona, bounces through a wireless net-

Joe Hagan, "Tweet Science," *New York*, October 2, 2011. Copyright © 2011 by New York Media LLC. All rights reserved. Reproduced by permission.

work and pings around a maze of servers until it lands inside a batch of computers situated on the third floor of a seventies-era office building in San Francisco, corner of Folsom and 4th Street.

At the headquarters of Twitter, there is an open-air hive of cubicles and a large, light-filled common area where staffers in T-shirts and jeans congregate with matching silver MacBooks with bluebird logos on them. There is a five-tier cereal dispenser and several varieties of boutique coffee; communal dishes are piled in a sink. On a marker board near the exit, employees share their ideas for making the company more humane, writing "flexible" and "artful" and "be polite."

The company struggles with an interlocked set of existential questions, starting with the most basic one possible: What is Twitter?

All is not transparent, however. Floor three, the technological core of this unusual enterprise, is off-limits. A sign tells those with access to WATCH FOR TAILGATING. Behind the double doors, computer engineers, some 250 of them, Ph.D.'s from MIT [Massachusetts Institute of Technology] and Stanford and Caltech, are busy trying to make order of the 200 million tweets a day, cascades of text messages from McCain, President [Barack] Obama, and the pope; [singer] Justin Bieber and the Pakistani who heard U.S. commandos raid [terrorist] Osama bin Laden's house; [rapper] Kanye West and [Venezuelan President] Hugo Chávez and the man who pretends to be [actor] Nick Nolte all day. Back there, in an attempt to solve the inherent paradoxes at the core of Twitter's ambitions, computer algorithms are being developed to classify and assign values to every single tweet in the ever-chattering Rube Goldberg machine [after cartoonist and inventor Goldberg, known for devising complex machines to perform simple tasks] they created five years ago....

"People describe Twitter as a global consciousness," says Ryan Sarver, a fast-talking engineer who comes out of his third-floor sanctum to meet me in a conference room. Sarver, who is responsible for managing this chaotic flow, the so-called fire hose of tweets, says Twitter has only begun to take shape. "We're in the early life cycle of what the platform is," he says. "This is version one."

A Different Sort of TV

In Silicon Valley, Twitter is already legend, one of those once-a-decade sure things, on the level of Microsoft or Apple or Google or Facebook—that not only changes the nature of the world but eventually makes it hard to remember a world in which it didn't exist. The ambition, and some of the rhetoric, is [printing press inventor Johannes] Gutenberg-size, though instead of Bibles, there's [singer] Beyoncé.

"There are nearly 7 billion people on this planet," says Jack Dorsey, the company's co-founder and original genius. "And we are building Twitter for all of them. They evolve, and so do we."

Measured by the number of people who've joined the flock, Twitter's growth is indeed staggering—a 370 percent surge in users since 2009. In fact, it resembles nothing so much as Google a decade ago, and everyone here, along with the small army of venture capitalists whose millions are funding this laboratory, is aware of this fact, as well as the implied competition with social-media superstars like Facebook and Zynga that are promising to go public and make lots of Valley V.C.'s [venture capitalists] very rich. Google has launched an assault with Google+, a more controlled social world, equidistant from Facebook and Twitter, and thus a possible refuge for those who are disaffected by Twitter's chaotic news flow.

The intense pressure to convert Twitter into a profitable business, and before a tech bubble pops, is palpable here. And it's happening as the company struggles with an interlocked set of existential questions, starting with the most basic one possible: What is Twitter? Initially, the idea was of a kind of adrenalized Facebook, with friends communicating with friends in short bursts—and indeed, Facebook rushed to borrow Twitter's innovations so it wouldn't be left behind. But as Twitter grew, it finally became clear to Twitter's brain trust that the relevant analogy was not a social network but a broadcast system—the birth of a different sort of TV.

They call it an "information network." "It did take a while to bring everybody around to that particular vision," says Twitter co-founder Ev Williams. "Over the last year or so is when that started to be more clear publicly."

But this revelation both simplified and complicated things. Where Facebook could keep aiming to be a comfortable place for people to hang out, Twitter's job would be to broker a connection between an audience and the talent, while also paneling itself with lucrative advertising, unobtrusively enough that the audience would not tune out. And currently, neither audience nor talent nor, especially, advertisers are anywhere near where they need to be for Twitter to make good on the immense expectations under which it is laboring.

Unlike a news or social site, where authors and their data are clearly delineated, the Twitter experience is much more difficult to aggregate.

At Twitter, where anxiety and optimism are never far from one another, the leadership is surprisingly frank about these problems. To start with, the audience is alarmingly fickle. Nielsen estimated that user-retention rates were around 40 percent. Twitter was easy to use at an entry level, but after a while it was hard for some people to see the point. Twitter has claimed as many as 175 million registered users, but numbers leaked to the online news site Business Insider in March [2011] put the number of actual people using it closer to 50 million, correcting for dead and duplicate accounts, automated "bots" and spam.

"There's this big gap, no doubt about it, between awareness of Twitter and engaged on Twitter," says Dick Costolo, Twitter's CEO [chief executive officer], a former improv comedian whose bald head and square-framed glasses give him the look of a walking exclamation point. When I meet him, he comes dashing into a corner office, apologizing for having initially canceled our interview as the company raced to process a new round of financing, $400 million from the Russian billionaire and highly regarded venture capitalist Yuri Milner—more money, more pressure. Costolo, along with Dorsey, who was pushed out two years ago and then returned, [late Apple cofounder] Steve Jobs-like, to try to take the company to the next level, are in charge of keeping the people in their seats. "This is probably our biggest product challenge, and the thing that Jack and I talk about the most," says Costolo. . . .

Much More Difficult to Aggregate

This summer, Twitter reengineered its search engine so it would value the "influence" of its users to better organize search results—to automatically bring up what [broadcast journalists] Brian Williams and Wolf Blitzer said about Libya as opposed to what somebody's crackpot uncle or [fitness personality] Richard Simmons said. Already, Twitter has tried to use interest-based "lists" to funnel people into thematic silos, an attempt to improve on the relatively primitive hashtag, the ubiquitous symbol for organizing ideas on Twitter. But unlike a news or social site, where authors and their data are clearly delineated, the Twitter experience is much more difficult to aggregate.

"At a simplistic level, it sounds easy," says Costolo, "because we could just go find, you know, the top trending topics and the tweet that was retweeted the most in the last two hours and show people that. But you want to be able to surface discovery at the global scale—'Hey, there's fomenting revolution in Tunisia'—but also surface discovery at the hyperlocal level: 'I can tell by the fact that you're on your iPhone, and you've exposed your lat-long [your location, as latitude and longitude] to me that you're at the Giants game, and here are a bunch of other tweets and pictures people are tweeting from the game right now.'"

The danger of overstructuring the information, he says, is that the user stops experiencing Twitter the way people originally came to experience Twitter, as the place for free-form, serendipitous chatter.

"You lose the roar of the crowd," says Costolo. "You look at the search results and 'Oh, there was a goal,' but you lose the athletes you follow and [chef] Mario Batali and Dennis Crowley from Foursquare. It's a design and engineering challenge.

Twitter is learning that it has to tend the talent as carefully as any entertainment company.

"This will be built into Twitter," he promises, "as a way of reducing the distance between awareness and engagement."

As it happens, that's the exact distance between Twitter as a phenomenon you've heard of and Twitter as a huge money-making business.

An Advertising Model Still in the Dream Stage

But to surface the content, and keep the audience happy, you have to make sure that the content keeps flowing in, and this, too, is far from a sure thing. A study conducted by sociologists working for Yahoo found that if they looked at a random Twitter user's feed, roughly 50 percent of the tweets came from one of just 20,000 users.[1] "It's really dominated by this media-celebrity-blogger elite," says Duncan Watts, one of the researchers. "It's a small number of users who are hyperconnected, and then there's everybody else just paying attention to those people."

To continue the broadcast metaphor, these people are the show users came to see. And Twitter is learning that it has to tend the talent as carefully as any entertainment company. In the planning rooms of Twitter, the most prolific and widely followed tweeters are called "influencers," or "power users," and they are at the core of its business. If it loses them, it becomes, essentially, MySpace—a digital graveyard where a party used to be. So while they race to retool the tweeting experience for the masses, Costolo and Dorsey are on a parallel campaign to keep Twitter's star attractions, celebrities and politicians and the media, chattering away on Twitter. Last year, they opened offices in Hollywood and Washington, D.C., hiring liaisons to act as free Twitter consultants and keep influencers pumping out all-star tweets. In a conference room around the corner from Costolo's office, Omid Ashtari, a former agent at Los Angeles talent firm Creative Artists Agency, tells me the pitch he gave actor James Franco before the Oscars last spring: "If you're on Twitter and you have a spotlight shining on you in other media, your Twitter resonance and your Twitter growth explodes."

The reason Twitter wants James Franco tweeting is to sell his audience to advertisers. And if it can figure out how to insert a Starbucks tweet into the Francosphere, and prompt people to buy coffee without stifling their intimacy with Franco, Twitter wins. This advertising model is still in the dream stage. But what a dream it is.

1. This article has been clarified to show that Yahoo's research findings were in reference to single Twitter accounts, not all users, and that they did not find that 50 percent of all tweets originated with those 20,000 users.

"A new kind of advertising that can go everywhere, frictionlessly, immediately," says Costolo. "It's not just a browser ad, it's not just a desktop ad, it goes to smart phones, it goes to feature phones, it can go to SMS [text messages], it can go to TV."

In theory, it's an ad-sponsored tweet that would go everywhere you want to be, cozied up with your friend James Franco like Texaco was with [comedian] Milton Berle 60 years ago.

But while they're doing all this blue-sky dreaming, the noise outside their windows is getting very loud. And Twitter is still recovering from self-inflicted wounds: The founders and early funders fought a pitched battle for months over what the company should be and who should run it. As one venture capitalist in Silicon Valley observes, it looked like the founders "drove their clown car into a gold mine and fell in."

Dorsey, a young engineer who came up with the idea of Twitter and helped build the prototype, was pushed out three years ago in a feud with co-founder Williams, its first funder and chairman, just as Twitter was becoming popular. The board of directors made Williams the leader, but after two years, Williams stepped down, evidently overwhelmed by the job. The board then handed the reins to Costolo, who had been advising Williams, and, in a bizarre about-face, brought Dorsey back six months ago as the new front man and chief product manager. Williams and a third co-founder, Biz Stone, who are still board members, decamped to start a new venture.

It's all happening a little too fast. "We've certainly resonated with a lot of people," says Dorsey. "But does that mean that we've arrived and can never go down? Absolutely not." . . .

The Gold May Be Lost Forever

Based on speculative secondary markets for private shares sold by former employees, the company is currently valued at $8 billion. But with more than 650 employees to support, and income projections for this year well below $200 million, it's not yet clear how it gets from here to there. In August, the company raised another $400 million and used it to buy out early investors, a sign that some money is already being taken off the table.

If too much dreck pours in, in the way of self-promoting tweets and obtrusive advertising, the gold may be lost forever.

"They've got ahead of themselves in their private valuations in the secondary market," says John Battelle, a technology journalist who heads high-tech marketing company Federated Media and is a friend and neighbor of Costolo's in Marin County, north of San Francisco. Perception of Twitter in the Valley is that it's fragile. One Twitter investor who has not yet cashed out told me, "There's a lot of head-scratching. They look at Twitter's numbers, and they say, 'That's all they can do with that?'"

"The criticisms of the company are very loud," acknowledges Fred Wilson. "A lot of people don't take the time to understand Twitter for what it really is."

Unfortunately, what it still is is a gold mine without, as yet, any sure way of getting the gold. And if too much dreck pours in, in the way of self-promoting tweets and obtrusive advertising, the gold may be lost forever. For Twitter, it's a hazardous paradox. As [actor] Ashton Kutcher recently said, "There's a danger of it becoming spammy, and that's what really hurt MySpace. . . . If Twitter doesn't apply the proper filters, it'll be harder to find the information you want. With Facebook, I'm probably not going to get spammed from my aunt or my best friend."

What's great about Twitter, as opposed to its competitors Google+ and Facebook, is that it's a free-for-all, with few rules, welcoming anyone and anything—it can be unpredictable and wild. But the danger is the Wild West becomes so many digital strip malls. And who'd want to spend time there?

> *They have a TV-radio problem. . . . How do you monetize TV? Nobody remembers who the first CEO of radio or TV was.*

Twitter, distracted by technology problems and infighting among its founders, was practically the last to understand that curation and filtering is part of its business. At first, it was happy to let users, and start-up developers, take care of it. One of the early attempts to focus Twitter was StockTwits, cofounded by an angel investor named Howard Lindzon. He used the symbol of two dollar signs, $$, as a code that users could add to their tweets, allowing Lindzon to sift for $$-related tweets and invent a separate conversation band for traders and businesspeople. "Curation and discovery is everything," says Lindzon. "Otherwise it's the dumbest product you've ever seen in your life."

Consequently, Lindzon has managed to peel away a whole thread of valuable conversation from Twitter. And he wasn't the only one: TweetDeck, a popular platform for monitoring Twitter, marshaled Twitter's users into its interface and was on its way to selling ads—until Twitter realized this was its business and paid $40 million to acquire TweetDeck in May. People like Lindzon, whose company is built on Twitter, believe Twitter is an invention akin to TV, an amazing development, but not worth anything without defined channels like his. "They have a TV-radio problem," says Lindzon. "How do you monetize TV? Nobody remembers who the first CEO of radio or TV was."

The Power and Greatest Weakness of Twitter

[Reality television star] Nicole Polizzi, A.K.A. @Snooki: "When your ass and chest is on fire cuz you used too much tingle in the tanning bed #GuiDeTTeProblems!!!"

This is the power and the greatest weakness of Twitter: the irresistible urge to advertise oneself. The impulse to make life a publicly annotated experience has blurred the distinction between advertising and self-expression, marketing and identity. Everyone is a celebrity, in the same stream. Marketers, too. And behind the scenes, advertisers are using an interface you're unlikely to see: a "dashboard" for watching you watch them, the online back room where Volkswagen and Virgin America and RadioShack and Starbucks are tracking their attempts to inject themselves into the conversation. This dashboard shows "how many times you're mentioned, how many people are following you, and a key measure, how many people are unfollowing you," explains a Twitter employee while demonstrating the dashboard on a silver MacBook in a conference room one morning in July.

This is the staging ground for making Twitter into a multibillion-dollar company. An advertiser like Starbucks or VW can buy access to different parts of the Twitter experience, placing its messages atop the list of the most-tweeted hashtags, or inside the Twitter feeds of people who already follow the brand, have a friend who does, or simply tweet about a related subject. Soon there will be a self-serve option, allowing smaller advertisers to sign up and instantly get into the mix. In every case, companies can monitor the response with a Twitter stock chart, the zigs and zags of how many clicks, replies, and retweets (when a tweet is passed along) are coming in. If nobody's responding, the ad disappears.

The idea is that by studying how people are reacting to a message, advertisers can experiment with different voices, personalities, pitches, and ideas and calibrate the tweet so the

Twitter charts keep going up and not down. Adam Bain, a former News Corp. advertising executive who is now Twitter's head of global revenue, describes it as "transparent" marketing.

> *Twitter needs mass scale, to "surface" all manner of customers to advertisers in a predictable and measurable way.*

Or maybe just more stealthy. In January, Audi promoted a Twitter hashtag in a Super Bowl TV ad, telling people to go to Twitter and talk about what the concept "progress" meant to them, using the hashtag #progressis. As the hashtag went viral, Audi's message was circulated through a kind of conversational side door. "Essentially, when you went to the Twitter site, you saw almost the whole world entering a conversation about a concept, progress," says Bain. "And Audi owned this concept of progress on Twitter for months."

The goal is to make advertisers members of the influencer class, cultivating the same credibility as Kutcher and Obama and getting Twitter users to retweet them as they would a friend. "Part of the magic for us is getting marketers to be in that center," Bain says, "and making them some of the most influential, because they have interesting things to say. . . . The amazing thing is that people are retweeting messages from marketers at a really large rate, and it's uniquely Twitter."

Twitter wants to be a place where the distance between celebrities and brands shrinks to next to nothing, where retweeting an advertisement is practically a function of who you are.

Twitter's model harks back to the early days of television, when the shows were the ads. In a way, it's a simpler world. Reality-TV socialite Kim Kardashian charged $10,000 a tweet to promote a product to her then—2 million followers ("Check out my commercial for @carlsjr. . . . What do you think?"). To convince advertisers to pay Twitter, and not Kim

Kardashian, Twitter needs mass scale, to "surface" all manner of customers to advertisers in a predictable and measurable way, over and above what they can achieve with one or two celebrity Twitter feeds. Twitter's not there yet.

"They don't have sufficient scale to make them a meaningful first-tier player in the social-media landscape," says John Battelle. "I can go to Yahoo, Microsoft, even Federated Media, and I can get tens of thousands of people I care about on a schedule I care about with returns on investment that I can optimize.

"The real business that needs to scale is the promoted tweets," continues Battelle. "How you get the right promoted tweets in front of the right person at the right time—it's the same problem as surfacing the content.". . .

Maybe Not Quite $8 Billion Big

Which brings us back to the folks on the third floor and the problem of making hash of all those tweets. If they can get more people to show up, stick around, and organize themselves inside a more streamlined and unified Twitter, it will give advertisers a bigger "inventory" of timelines within which to insert their messages. It also strengthens what Twitter calls its users' "interest graphs," allowing advertisers to target them with precision through their matrix of comments and replies and friends and followers, not unlike how a Google ad finds you through your own search. If you like Snooki, for instance, you might also enjoy a tweet from a tanning-lotion company in your timeline. Or a tweet about another MTV reality show, *16 and Pregnant*. Or one about Wonderful Pistachios, the nuts she got paid to promote on TV.

Or not. Twitter has proved valuable for aggregating real-time news, or snarking about celebrities on TV—two pretty big businesses, but maybe not quite $8 billion big and certainly not enough to meet the Earth-size ambitions Dorsey has in mind.

Lindzon says Twitter is the "greatest invention in the history of the Internet," but he is skeptical that Twitter can organize that entire vat of 200 million tweets a day into a fluid and orderly experience, billboard it with advertisements, and still retain its biggest strength—which is surprise. "I want to have that 'aha' moment," he says. "If they can figure out how to monetize that, good luck."

10

Twitterish

John McWhorter

John McWhorter is a linguist, contributing editor to The New Republic, *and author of numerous books on language and race, including* What Language Is (And What It Isn't and What It Could Be) *and* The Power of Babel: A Natural History of Language.

First used to categorize tweets, the hashtag symbol on Twitter gives irony or mockery to what is said. And like slang from texting and instant messaging, the hashtag has entered everyday conversation, criticized widely as an erosion of English writing skills. Nonetheless, written conventions routinely become a part of speech. E-mail, texting, and Twitter have dramatically changed communication—the separation of casual speaking and formal writing—and writing has become a form of talk itself. The hashtag also reflects this change, resembling speech in its tone, casualness, and immediacy. Besides, like other expressions before it, the hashtag is a passing trend that will not harm the English language.

One has lately heard much of the hashtag. That is, the Twitter symbol #, used to categorize a tweet. Charlie Sheen's first tweet, for example, was famously: "Winning..! Choose your Vice . . . #winning #chooseyourvice." #Winning has gone on to live in irony across the Twitterverse, in mockery of the eternally less-than-winning Sheen. But even

John McWhorter, "Twitterish," *The New Republic*, June 22, 2012. Copyright © 2012 by The New Republic. All rights reserved. Reproduced by permission.

President Obama recently urged students to tweet their senators about raising the interest rates on federally subsidized student loans with the hashtag "#DontDoubleMyRate."

The new thing, however, is using the word "hashtag" in conversation. Especially if you are under a certain age, you may be catching people saying things like, "I ran into that guy I met—hashtag happy!" or, in response to someone complaining, "My flashlight app isn't working," perhaps you have heard the retort, "Hashtag First World problems!" A college student not long ago reported a favorite witticism to be appending observations with: "Hashtag did that just happen?"

Given that Twitter, along with texting and instant-messaging, is so often thought of as a dire threat to the writing skills of the American adults of tomorrow—not to mention to the English language and therefore civilization itself—what in the world does it mean that people are now speaking in Twitter? Not much, actually. Twitter may be changing the way we talk but not in a way that is cause for concern. In other words: Hashtag chill out.

The spoken hashtag is part of a general trend—one rarely treated as a scourge, generally barely perceived, and actually a sign of the zeitgeist. I refer to a tendency to frame ourselves in conversation as performers, from an ironic distance, in a way that would have been impossible before movies and television began to deeply permeate modern life. "Hashtag happy" elicits a mental picture of the speaker viewed from a distance, labeled with the word happy. Think of the way someone often describes having received great news while miming a holler, "Yeah!"—pumping his fist, putting on the grimace one would have while actually yelling, but uttering the cheer sotto voce. It's a cheer in quotation marks—a cheer framed and viewed from afar. One could not do this without living and breathing film and television as we do. What reason would a rainforest tribesman have to depict himself cheering with the volume turned down?

Nor is it unusual for written conventions to make their way into speech. Acronyms are rife in modern speech: VIP, NATO, NGO, MILF. Then there are expressions such as "e.g." and "i.e." and "with a capital . . ."—all of which are so well-established that they feel like speech to most of us. But they emerged from writing and would make no sense without it. It's not intuitive for illiterate people to break words down into isolated sounds or letters, as acronyms require; they are more likely to sense that words are composed of syllables, that is, chunks of sounds.

Many might feel that there is something different about the spoken hashtag—that it seems slangier than "e.g." and so many other expressions. It's one thing when people say things like, "It was just a mess, period," pronouncing a punctuation mark, but something different when people start bringing texting's "LOL"—"laughing out loud"—into spoken language, along with the even cuddlier version "lolz." The former seems like tipping our cap to blackboard stringencies; the latter may seem like mussing someone's hair after they've already been out in the wind—isn't casual speech messy enough already? There is a point worth noting here, but not one too dramatic or revolutionary.

The spoken hashtag is very much a sign of our times: Americans are talking like writing once again—but predictably for our increasingly oral and informal era, the writing being talked is essentially a form of talk itself.

This brings out another reason the spoken hashtag is less insidious than it seems. In their brevity, their tendency toward the spontaneous, their subjectivity, and often their pungency, texting and Twitter are a lot like speech—and in fact, are only writing in the technical sense. Back in the day, there was usually a casual language learned unconsciously on mother's knee and a formal language acquired more carefully in school and from books. However, if there is casual speaking and formal writing, then one can imagine that there might be some bleed, such as with formal speaking. All societies exhibit this tendency to at least some extent. Homer, whose works were chanted in all their elaboration from memory and were only later committed to writing, is one example. In the United States, there was old-fashioned oratory of the "Four score and seven years ago" variety, for which audiences used to turn out and in which schoolchildren were trained.

However, in modern America, talking the way we write is a marginal practice. The flowery speeches of old are no more, and, even when we give formal addresses, they are more conversational than William Jennings Bryan could have ever imagined. What we manifest, however, and quite often, is the other kind of possible "bleed": writing the way we talk. It used to be that letters and notes were about all there was in this category. Today, however, e-mail, texts, and now Twitter have changed communication profoundly. And, in their come-as-you-are atmosphere, hashtags are writing in the physical sense but speech in their tone, immediacy, and shagginess. The spoken hashtag is very much a sign of our times: Americans are talking like writing once again—but predictably for our increasingly oral and informal era, the writing being talked is essentially a form of talk itself.

And, as talk goes, the whole spoken hashtag business is likely a passing trend. Fifty years from now, clever obsessives will consider it anachronistic when someone uses a spoken hashtag in a movie set in 2018. All eras have their ways of being cutely ironic, and all leave the language no worse for wear. In the old days, there was the "Calling . . ." expression—"Calling Dr. Freud!" to comment on someone's seeming neurosis—or the recent ". . . much?" formulation. "Obsessive much?" asks the friend of the person wondering whether she should iron her socks.

It wasn't so long ago that the scourge of civilization was supposed to be the informal writing used by people composing e-mails. Thanks to "thx" and other similar abbreviations, yesterday's handwringers foresaw doom. The response to this today would seem to be: "#Sotenminutesago." Language marches on, proud and unafraid.

Organizations to Contact

The editors have compiled the following list of organizations concerned with the issues debated in this book. The descriptions are derived from materials provided by the organizations. All have publications or information available for interested readers. The list was compiled on the date of publication of the present volume; names, addresses, phone and fax numbers, and e-mail and Internet addresses may change. Be aware that many organizations take several weeks or longer to respond to inquiries, so allow as much time as possible.

American Library Association (ALA)
50 E. Huron, Chicago, IL   60611
(800) 545-2433
website: www.ala.org

The American Library Association (ALA) is the oldest and largest library association in the world, with more than sixty-five thousand members. Its mission is to promote the highest quality library and information services and public access to information. ALA offers professional services and publications to members and nonmembers. The association supports the use of social networking sites in libraries and classrooms as a part of economic, civic, and cultural life.

Berkman Center for Internet & Society
Harvard Law School, 23 Everett St., 2nd Floor
Cambridge, MA   02138
(617) 495-7547 • fax: (617) 495-7641
e-mail: cyber@law.harvard.edu
website: cyber.law.harvard.edu

The Berkman Center for Internet & Society was founded to study cyberspace and contribute to its development. Its primary activities include research and investigation of the boundaries in cyberspace between government, businesses, commerce, and education, and the relationship of the law to each of these areas. Its website includes a monthly newsletter, podcasts, and publications on such topics of interest as social media and its impacts.

Center for Democracy and Technology (CDT)
1634 I St. NW, #1100, Washington, DC   20006
(202) 637-9800
website: www.cdt.org

CDT's mission is to develop public policy solutions that advance constitutional civil liberties and democratic values in new computer and communications media. Pursuing its mission through policy research, public education, and coalition building, the center works to increase citizens' privacy and the public's control over the use of personal information held by government and other institutions. Its publications include issue briefs, policy papers, and CDT "Policy Posts."

Center for Safe and Responsible Internet Use (CSRIU)
474 W. 29th Ave., Eugene, OR   97405
e-mail: info@embracecivility.org
website: www.embracecivility.org/

Through its program Embrace Civility in the Digital Age, the Center for Safe and Responsible Internet Use (CSRIU) provides research and outreach services to address issues of the safe and responsible use of the Internet. It provides guidance to parents, educators, librarians, policymakers, and others regarding effective strategies to assist young people in gaining the knowledge, skills, motivation, and self-control to use the Internet and other information technologies in a safe and responsible manner.

Electronic Frontier Foundation (EFF)
454 Shotwell St., San Francisco, CA   94110-1914
(415) 436-9333 • fax: (415) 436-9993
e-mail: information@eff.org
website: www.eff.org

The Electronic Frontier Foundation (EFF) is an organization of professionals, students, and other individuals that seeks to promote a better understanding of telecommunications issues. It fosters awareness of civil liberties issues arising from advancements in computer-based communications and supports litigation to preserve, protect, and extend First Amendment rights in computing and telecommunications technologies. EFF's publications include the electronic newsletter *EFFector Online*, online bulletins, and publications, including *Know Your Digital Rights' Guide: Guard Against 4th Amendment Violations*.

Electronic Privacy Information Center (EPIC)

1718 Connecticut Ave. NW, Suite 200, Washington, DC 20009
(202) 483-1140 • fax: (202) 483-1248
website: www.epic.org

As an advocate of the public's right to electronic privacy, EPIC sponsors educational and research programs, compiles statistics, and conducts litigation pertaining to privacy and other civil liberties. Its publications include the biweekly electronic newsletter *EPIC Alert*.

Federal Trade Commission (FTC)

600 Pennsylvania Ave. NW, Washington, DC 20580
(202) 326-2222
website: www.ftc.gov

The Federal Trade Commission (FTC) deals with issues that touch the economic life of every American. It aims to prevent business practices that are anti-competitive, deceptive, or unfair to consumers. Its website offers information on online privacy and security issues as well as protecting kids online and on social networks. With other federal agencies, the FTC maintains OnGuardOnline.gov, the federal government's website designed to help US citizens be safe, secure, and responsible online.

Internet Society (ISOC)
1775 Wiehle Ave., Suite 102, Reston, VA   20190-5108
(703) 326-2120 • fax: (703) 326-9881
e-mail isoc@isoc.org
website: www.internetsociety.org

A group of technologists, developers, educators, researchers, government representatives, and businesspeople, Internet Society (ISOC) supports the development and dissemination of standards for the Internet and works to ensure global cooperation and coordination for the Internet and related Internet-working technologies and applications. In tandem with the Internet Engineering Task Force (IETF), it publishes the *IETF Journal*, the *Internet Society Newsletter*, regular columns, annual reports, and various other publications.

Bibliography

Books

Ben Agger
Oversharing: Presentations of Self in the Internet Age. New York: Routledge, 2011.

Lori Andrews
I Know Who You Are and I Saw What You Did: Social Networks and the Death of Privacy. New York: Free Press, 2012.

Nancy K. Baym
Personal Connections in the Digital Age. Malden, MA: Polity, 2010.

Nicholas Carr
The Shallows: What the Internet Is Doing to Our Brains. New York: W.W. Norton, 2010.

Nicholas A. Christakis and James H. Fowler
Connected: The Surprising Power of Our Social Networks and How They Shape Our Lives. New York: Little, Brown, and Company, 2009.

Viktor Mayer-Schonberger
Delete: The Virtue of Forgetting in the Digital Age. Princeton, NJ: Princeton University Press, 2009.

Deborah Micek and Warren Whitlock
Twitter Revolution: How Social Media and Mobile Marketing Is Changing the Way We Do Business & Market Online. Las Vegas, NV: Xeno Press, 2008.

Evgeny Morozov
The Net Delusion: The Dark Side of Internet Freedom. New York: Public Affairs, 2011.

Zizi Papacharissi   *A Networked Self: Identity, Community, and Culture on Social Network Sites.* New York: Routledge, 2011.

Sherry Turkle   *Alone Together: Why We Expect More from Technology and Less from Each Other.* New York: Basic Books, 2011.

Periodicals and Internet Sources

Owen Barder   "Twitter: Society's New Dial Tone," *Owen Abroad*, December 5, 2011. www.owen.org.

Kiley Bense   "Is Twitter Killing the English Language?" *The Isis*, May 7, 2012. http://isismagazine.org.uk.

Karry Carlat   "Confessions of a Tweeter," *New York Times*, November 11, 2011.

Golnaz Esfandiari   "The Twitter Devolution," *Foreign Policy*, June 7, 2010.

Paul Farhi   "The Twitter Explosion," *American Journalism Review*, April/May 2009.

Malcolm Gladwell   "Small Change," *New Yorker*, October 4, 2010.

Stephen Johnson   "How Twitter Will Change the Way We Live," *Time*, June 5, 2009.

Nathan Jurgenson   "Why Chomsky Is Wrong About Twitter," *Salon*, October 23, 2011. www.salon.com.

Shira Ovide "Twitter's Slow Road to IPO," *Wall Street Journal*, March 2, 2012.

Kathleen Parker "The Twitter Phenomenon—In Touch, Always, in Cyberspace," *Washington Post*, December 3, 2008.

Sunsara Taylor "The Culture That Killed Tyler Clementi," *The World Can't Wait*, October 7, 2010. www.worldcantwait.net.

Neil Tweedie "Are Twitter and Facebook Affecting How We Think?" *Telegraph*, June 28, 2010.

Ben Zimmer "Twitterology: A New Science?" *New York Times*, October 29, 2011.

Ethan Zuckerman "A Twitter Revolution?" *Foreign Policy*, January 14, 2011.

Index

F

Face-to-face contact, 11–12
Facebook
    adult use of, 7
    awareness of, 63
    ease of use, 14
    in Iran, 39–40
    news and reporting on, 48
    Twitter *vs.*, 8, 71–72, 77–78
    work relationships and, 15
Fader, Peter, 65–66
Federated Media, 81
Followers on Twitter, 13–16
Forte, Andrea, 7
Franco, James, 75

G

Global Language Monitoring Survey, 17
Global Voices Online, 40
Goldberg, Rube, 70
Golvin, Charles, 21
Google (search engine), 23, 65, 81
Google+ (social networking), 71, 78
Greenfield, Susan, 17, 34, 35–36
Gutenberg, Johannes, 71

H

Hagan, Joe, 69–82
Hart, Melissa, 54–60
Harvard Law School, 42
Harvard University, 39
Hashtag usage
    with advertising, 80
    Tweet rates with, 79

as Twitter symbol, 73
usage in Twitter, 83–87
Hatetweet, 32
Hierarchy of needs (Maslow), 27–28
Hosanagar, Kartik, 65
Hunt, Tara, 22, 24

I

Industrial Revolution, 27
Interactive Telecommunications Program (NYU), 26
International Center on Nonviolent Conflict, 41
Iran, 7, 38–41
Irelan, Ryan, 20–21
Islamic Republic, 46

J

Jelliffe, Pete, 23
Jones, Hessie, 8–9, 8n3
Jugnoo company, 8

K

Kao, John, 32
Kardashian, Kim, 80–81
Kierkegaard, Søren, 30
KnowledgeWharton (online business journal), 61–68
Kutcher, Aston, 65–66, 77, 80

L

Laing, R.D., 36–37
Lavallee, Andrew, 19–24
Lewis, David, 28
Lincoln College, 34